Acting
Face to Face

THE ACTOR'S GUIDE TO UNDERSTANDING
HOW YOUR FACE COMMUNICATES EMOTION
FOR TV & FILM

REVISED & EXPANDED 2ND EDITION

By John Sudol

Copyright © 2013, 2021 John Sudol

All rights reserved. No portion of the book may be reproduced or utilized in any form or by any means, electronic or mechanical, including photocopying, recording, or by any other information storage and retrieval system, without permission in writing from John Sudol.

Edited by

First Edition
Lisa Martel

Second Edition
Leslie Hough

https://www.emotiontrainingcenter.com/books
https://www.emotiontrainingcenter.com/store
https://www.emotiontrainingcenter.com/etc-licensing

Contents

Message from John 1

About the Acting: Face to Face Series 4

How I Lost the Job 9

Acting: An Art of Deception 15

Who's Getting All the On-Camera Work and Why? 25

The Secret Language Your Face Speaks 39

Why Your Facial Messages May Not Reach Others the Way You Intend 77

Myths and Misconceptions about On-Camera Acting 97

Emotional Alignment: Are You In or Out? 127

The Mini Emotion Screen Test 137

Emotional Alignment: Your Path to On-Camera Success 171

About the Author 183

Acknowledgments 185

Bibliography 187

"How can we remember our ignorance, which our growth requires, when we are using our knowledge all the time?" – Henry Thoreau

"Create your own method. Don't depend slavishly on mine. Make up something that will work for you! But keep breaking traditions, I beg you…" – Constantine Stanislavsky

"The actor must understand the complexity of emotional experience in attempting to convey an emotion in performance. The discussion of deception may help him prevent his personal feelings from leaking through in his performance. When the actor is feeling his way into the emotional experience of a character, he needs to be sure that his expression of that emotion is commonly understood. " – Dr. Paul Ekman

In loving memory of my father Jack and brother Gary, who left us all far too soon. I wish I could have seen their faces when reading this book...

Other books and online course by John Sudol:

Ebook/Paperback: Acting: Face to Face 2: Emotional Alignment

Emotional Alignment Course:
www.emotiontrainingcenter.com

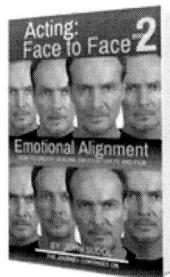 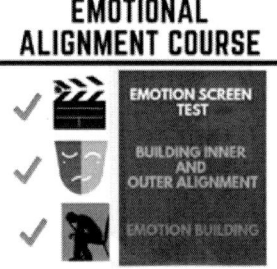 

Acting:
Face to Face

THE ACTOR'S GUIDE TO UNDERSTANDING
HOW YOUR FACE COMMUNICATES EMOTION
FOR TV & FILM

REVISED & EXPANDED 2ND EDITION

By John Sudol

Message from John

I would like to take a few moments to share some of my thoughts about the current times and this second edition. I promise I'll be brief.

When Acting Face to Face first came out 2013, I received a lot of great feedback from actors, directors, managers and casting directors, it also became a #1 Best Seller on Amazon. And, Backstage named it one of "Eleven Amazing Books for the On-Camera Actor."

I've received hundreds of e-mails from actors all over the country and around the world. Many were congratulatory. Some were more personal and often quite moving. I heard from actors who went into great detail about the struggles, frustrations and disappointments they experienced while working on-camera, as well as the relief they felt on knowing that what they suspected was missing could be recaptured. All of the support, acknowledgment and praise has meant a great deal to me.

However, what I've found most interesting was that the positive feedback was not only from actors and others in the movie making industry, the book was reaching a whole new audience. This new audience included financial managers, CEOs, tech entrepreneurs and salespeople, which makes absolute sense. These are all people who rely on their facial communication to lead and inspire their teams, clients and investors.

As I write this, we are still in the middle of the pandemic, waiting for the vaccine to be distributed. It's been a horrible year for so many with illness, jobs lost, production stopped and being stuck at home. If we choose to go out, we must wear a mask. Now the thing about masks, masks keep us safe, but they also, of course, cover many of the facial muscle groups that we utilize to communicate effectively. Relying solely on the eyes to determine what someone is thinking or feeling has led to more frustration than communication. It is also a prime example of how hard it is to read someone when all you have is the eyes.

In this new second edition, I have revised the "Myths and Misconceptions" chapter and I investigate those challenges of mask-wearing. I also go deeper into EYE COMMUNICATION - what the eyes can say and what they can't.

The science of emotion and facial expression is constantly expanding and I have continued researching. This is reflected in updates throughout the book. I've also added over 35 new photos to illustrate specificity and subtlety of emotional expression. But, the biggest change is the addition of 3 NEW chapters. Two of these chapters are dedicated solely to a mini version of my proprietary Emotion Screen Test (EST)*. I wanted to give all those who read this book something specific to take away- action steps that will give greater insight into how you create and reveal emotion on a truly personal level.

The EST is a guided in-depth self-evaluation of your own facial expressions. Its main purpose is to help you clearly evaluate your emotion creating and revealing strengths and weaknesses. The "aha" moments that almost always come from doing the EST (even the short one) can be an incredible motivator for further, deeper work.

Most of all, I want to emphasize that I have written this book for you. I want nothing more than for you to succeed in your career goals. For me, it's never been about achieving massive fame and fortune, but rather achieving true understanding of how we all communicate. It's about doing really creative, relatable work of which we can be really proud. So, thanks to you for joining me here. We are going to work together in this process to make you a stronger, more confident, and ultimately more entertaining and moving storyteller, and to me that's the greatest success.

Game On!

John Sudol
11/23/2020

About the Acting: Face to Face Series

How valuable would it be if you knew exactly how to trigger a specific emotion or combination of emotions and knew how intensely it was being revealed on your face?

What if you knew what these emotions looked and felt like – and how to make them bigger or smaller? More intense or less intense? What might that do for you on-camera acting career?

Contrary to some beliefs regarding on-camera acting, the camera doesn't magically place emotion or thought on your face - you do. Knowing how to use your face to communicate thought and feeling is a skill and often the difference between booking the on-camera job or not.

Acting: Face to Face is a two book series about learning how to speak what I call "The Language of the Face." When spoken correctly, you give the viewer permission to read your mind and instinctively understand the thoughts and emotions that you, as the character, are experiencing in the moment.

Designed primarily for on-camera acting, the goal of both books is to give greater clarity to this nonverbal language and the tools with which to speak it.

Book 1, Acting: Face to Face, *The Actor's Guide to Understanding How Your Face Communicates Emotion for TV & Film* is about identifying the real emotional facial communication challenges of on-camera acting. In Book 2, Acting: Face to Face 2, *Emotional Alignment*, I lay out a step by step process or blueprint for overcoming those challenges.

Some would argue that an actor's facial communication just happens naturally and training is not needed. I would have to respectfully disagree with that statement. Although emotions happen naturally in real life, a whole slew of challenges arise for many when you have to speak this facial language fluently, on demand and have it spring primarily from your imagination.

The Acting: Face to Face Series is not a remix of Stanislavski, Chekhov, Stella Adler, Strasberg, Meisner, or any other great acting teacher's work. In fact, it is an adjunct to those teachings. It's also not about how to be more committed to the craft of acting, marketing yourself or finding your acting spiritual center – although you just might. Leaning to speak the Language of the Face is a very specific aspect of on-camera acting. If you master it, your odds of having a successful on-camera acting career will be enormously increased.

The techniques found in both books are based on the work of leading researchers in the field of emotions, as well as years of trial and error working with thousands of actors – in my own acting studio, on the set and while I was in casting. Until now, an actor's training has focused on two means of emotional communication – the body and the voice. By incorporating how the face communicates thoughts, feelings and emotion and how it works in conjunction with the body and voice, a third dimension is added – forming what I call "The Emotional Triad."

In this first book, we'll focus on the main differences between stage and on-camera acting. We'll explore current beliefs, tools and adjustments, as well as some of the misconceptions about on-camera acting. I'll also introduce you to what I call "Emotional Alignment" – which defines the relationship between the intensity you feel internally and what is appearing on your face. This book also covers:

- Why only a small percentage of on-camera actors get the majority of the work
- What those actors do differently than the rest
- The science of emotions
- Introduction to "The Language of the Face" and The Emotional Triad"
- Understanding your own emotional distortions
- Identifying your emotion creating and revealing strengths and weaknesses
- The 4 steps to achieving "Emotional Alignment"

This book will also address some very important questions, such as:

- What is the difference between the training you received for the stage and training required for on-camera acting?
- Why has this difference not previously been taught?
- Why do certain actors have an easier time transitioning between stage and screen?
- Why doesn't "romantic language" inspire us all in the same way?

- Why do people see you differently than how you see yourself – and how critical is this awareness to your success?
- Why does your face remain blank even though you feel you're experiencing emotion intensely?
- Why does every thought, whether you want it to or not, register on your face?

If you're reading this book, you most likely have similar questions to the ones I've stated above, as well as some very specific questions about your personal emotional expressiveness. I'm confident that as you continue reading, you will find answers to many, if not all of your questions.

At the end of this new edition, I have included a mini version of my proprietary Emotion Screen Test. The goal of the mini Screen Test is for you to determine how effective your emotion creating and revealing skills are and to get a baseline from which to work. It includes how take the screen test, evaluate it and assess it.

In the last chapter, I give you a look into the next step of our journey together. There, I lay out the path to Emotional Alignment. I cover the adjustments you'll need to make, what new tools you'll need to acquire and the action steps you can take right now to increase your odds of being a successful on-camera actor.

I believe that the more you understand about how you reveal emotion personally, the nature of those emotions, and what they look like on your face from the most subtle to the extreme, the more dynamic a storyteller you will become.

The actor with the skill to create and control what their face communicates is the actor most suited to work in front of the camera.

Let the journey begin.

Chapter 1

How I Lost the Job

As a young actor, I was told that if I wanted to see who the good actors were, I should turn the sound off on my TV and just watch.

I did this often and it was very revealing. When the acting was good, I knew that the actors were feeling and expressing something – I could see it right there on their faces! I also knew that I wanted to aspire to this level of acting. I remember one of my acting teachers telling me to "work hard, perfect my craft, build my toolbox and it will happen – naturally and organically."

So, I did. I worked hard to fill my toolbox with what I thought I would need to be a successful actor. I would ultimately come to learn that something critical was missing- a tool required for all on-camera acting, a tool none of my acting teachers could give me, a tool I would have to learn on my own.

About 20 years ago, I was at an audition for a guest-starring role on a major network television show. I did my first read for the director and it went well. I could tell that the director liked me because he started to adjust what I was doing. As most of you know, this is a good sign. Whenever a director or casting director gives you direction, it usually means they like what you're doing and want to make adjustments for a second read. I remember he wanted a specific reaction from me at a specific time. To him, it was pivotal to moving the story ahead.

So, I did the scene again. He shook his head "no" – that wasn't quite it. Now I knew he really liked me because he came from behind the table, put his arm around me and started giving me what I call "romantic language." Before you jump to the wrong conclusion, I define the term "romantic language" as words or phrases designed to evoke an emotion or feeling similar to what the character is experiencing. For example, remember how you felt when your dog ran away or the first time you were heartbroken?

So, the director's purpose for this romantic language was to inspire some kind of emotional connection and reaction from me. His words were good. I was inspired. I was connected. I searched my memory banks for something I could use to reveal this moment. "Okay, I'm ready to go," I said, and did the scene again. When I was done, a long silence followed. Then a strained smile appeared on the director's face as he said, "Thanks." I was dismissed and the next actor was ushered in.

Sound familiar to anyone? Needless to say, I didn't book the job.

I walked out of the room completely frustrated. Now the thing is – I wasn't a beginner actor at the time. I had many guest-starring and lead credits. The job was mine; all I had to do was give him the reaction he wanted. And the strange part was I thought that's what I was doing. Then I realized, although I was a trained actor, nothing in my training had prepared me to interpret what that director was asking of me, turn it into something emotional and then reveal it on my face in a way that he could recognize.

As time went on, what got even clearer to me was that the director wasn't asking me to act differently, but to react in a very specific way. He didn't want me to do something with my body, which is what I was doing. He wanted to see it on my face. Not only did I fail to give it to him, a realization hit me for the very first time –

I didn't know how. I'm not saying that I didn't know how to react, I'm saying I didn't know how to react in the specific way he wanted.

To compound the problem further, he couldn't explain what he wanted from me in a way that I could understand. All I knew at the time was that he wanted to see specific thoughts manifest on my face and I just didn't know how to do that.

You guessed it – that was the tool that was missing – a way to interpret what he was asking of me and turn it into a visible, emotional reaction on my face.

Over the years, I have often thought about this as a secret, nonverbal, often non-physical language that all actors are expected to know. I know it exists! I saw it on TV the many times I turned the sound off. I saw the actor's inner thoughts and feelings. So, the question ultimately became, "How do you know it?" How do you specifically know what someone is thinking and feeling? Is there some kind of special telepathic communication from them to you?

To the untrained eye, it looks like they're not doing anything at all. Yet you intuitively know differently. So, what are you really seeing? What are those working actors doing differently than other actors? Can it really be learned?

The Turning Point

My determination and dedication to understanding what these actors were doing differently ultimately sent me on a twofold quest. One, most obvious, was to study those working actors for clues. Two, which is not so obvious, was to learn all I could about emotions. Why emotions? Because I knew intuitively that what was appearing on the faces of those actors were primarily emotional and/or cognitive responses to something.

Although I was in an art form and business that relies primarily on how we communicate facially, it quickly became clear to me how little I knew about emotions. So, to know how those actors were speaking this nonverbal emotional language, it made sense that I would need to learn all I could about emotions.

New Discovery

In the latter part of 2003, I stumbled upon the work of Dr. Paul Ekman, one of the leading researchers in the field of emotions. Studying his work and that of many other researchers changed my world. Everything I instinctively knew about how we communicate emotionally was now validated by science.

This field of science rocked my world in ways I never anticipated. It opened my eyes to so many things – like how we're all not wired or raised to express emotion in the same way. This explained why some actors have an advantage in creating and revealing emotion over others. I learned that there are universal emotions and unique facial expressions, triggers, impulses, and sensations associated with them.

What I also learned from the science was that when an emotion is triggered, there are not only physical changes to the body and the voice, but also muscular changes to the face. Most importantly, these facial muscular changes are universally recognized.

My quest ultimately paid off when I discovered that there was a way I could teach actors how to incorporate this science into their craft and attain what the top actors we watched with the sound off seemed to do so naturally.

If this message speaks to you and you're thinking that you'd like to acquire the skill that only a select group of actors have, you will have to be willing to experience a shift in thinking about acting, especially on-camera acting. This shift in thinking is not about using the old tools in a new way. It's about the birth of something new – a new set of skills that need to be added to your acting toolbox.

This is where *Acting: Face To Face* begins.

Chapter 2

Acting: An Art of Deception

When lies look like truth, you're not a liar but a... storyteller.

Many actors start out thinking that acting is a game of make-believe. While playing this game, they pretend they're someone they're not. They make believe they're doing something they normally wouldn't do. It's a wonderful pastime for children and it's fairly easy to do. The rules are very loose, and the goal is merely to enjoy the feeling you get from playing.

When playing make-believe, you don't have to be too concerned with the details of your imaginary world. You don't have to be concerned if your inner life is reflected in your body and voice, or on your face – or if you get caught playing the game. Although fun, the game is undisciplined and self-serving. And it doesn't evoke the powerful emotion and specific action an on-camera actor needs in order to be alive, engaging and believable.

Harold Clurman, the great director and theatre critic, once referred to good acting as "lies like truth." I wholeheartedly agree with Mr. Clurman. I believe he chose the word *lies* instead of *make-believe* very deliberately. Here's why.

For an on-camera actor, especially when auditioning for a role, you must be incredibly disciplined. Your imagined world must be very specific, filled with detailed information that must be, most importantly, conveyed to others in a way they understand and recognize. Every movement, vocal change and facial expression is thoroughly scrutinized by the viewer and the stakes are high if you're caught "playing."

Noted acting teacher, Stella Adler, echoes Clurman's words, "Every play is a fiction. It's the actor's job to de-fictionalize the fiction." We can easily change the word "play" to screenplay, TV script, sides, or copy to fit our purpose. According to Ms. Adler, the script is filled with facts and those facts are lies until the actor gets hold of them.

Deception is the result of turning lies into truth. However, if you don't know what lies you're telling or you don't tell them in a way that looks truthful, you'll never be able to achieve deception. It's the actor's job to understand, relate, motivate, and tell those lies in a way that looks like real life.

Unlike how we may lie to get out of a speeding ticket, the actor's deception is done with the viewer's knowledge and permission. In other words, your audience *wants* you to deceive them. They're giving you permission to do so each time they go to a movie theater or turn on the TV. Think about it, Tom Hanks isn't an astronaut – he never went to the moon, but he deceived us all.

Anthony Hopkins isn't a serial killer who eats his victims, but for a short while we believed he was. Meryl Streep wasn't the Prime Minster of England. She took the lies in the script and executed them so well that she won an Academy Award for her deception. The lies these actors told rang so truthfully with us that we thoroughly believed everything they said and did.

An audience will pay good money to have you deceive them, but they won't pay a cent if they catch you in the lie. So, no matter what acting philosophy you adhere to, if the viewer doesn't view your lies as the truth – game over.

When deception breaks down, lies are exposed.

The Truth about Lying

According to leading deception experts, lying entails the fabrication or distortion of information and an attempt to do so in a way that looks natural to avoid suspicion. At the same time, the truth must be kept concealed. Lying also involves creating and describing events that have not happened. Although this sounds like what actors are asked to do, it's not the same thing.

The difference between lying and acting is that an actor has permission to deceive and a liar does not. Both have a common goal – to be believed. And both share a common problem – keeping the truth concealed while appearing to be natural.

To be believed as an actor, you must skillfully pass off an imaginary world as the truth, while concealing the realities of who you *really* are and how you *really* feel. You must do this each time you audition for a role. However, these realities often leak out as a result of nerves, lack of clarity or lack of commitment to the task at hand. The leakage can manifest in many ways – unwanted physical movement and facial expressions, eye rolling, hard swallows, and excessive blinking, to name just a few.

I've seen this happen frequently when coaching actors for their auditions. Most are totally unaware that these things are happening until I bring it to their attention. You may be wondering how that's possible.

Well, here's something important to understand about lying – your brain doesn't like it. It's wired to work in accordance with the truth. When you lie – and it doesn't matter if it's an outright lie or a simple attempt to deceive – your brain has to deny reality.

We are not wired to lie, but to tell the truth.

In your attempt to reveal from the *imaginary* world, the *real* world will constantly try to have a say in it. This is because lying and deception takes a lot of brain activity. There's so much that needs to be invented, invested in, and remembered. In doing so, we often stop doing what we normally do – and start doing what we normally *wouldn't* do.

For example, if you normally use your hands a lot when you speak, the increased brain activity when you're lying will cause a reduction in hand movement. Another example may be an increase or decrease in facial expressions. These additions or subtractions to what you normally do are what professional gamblers call "tells". Almost everyone has them when they lie.

Most of our nonverbal tells are expressed through three channels – the voice, body and face. For the voice, there are vocal cues, tone, rhythm, and style. For the body, there are gestures, body posture, interpersonal space, touching, and gazing. And for the face, there are emotional and non-emotional expressions.

Since up to 93% of our communication is done through nonverbal channels, this is where most people get caught in a lie. So, understanding how you communicate nonverbally is paramount to achieving deception, as is being aware of your tells and working towards eliminating them.

You see, it's not only what you *do* that exposes the lie – it's also what you *don't do*. When we truly become emotional, there are natural changes to the voice, body and face. If these changes don't occur, your truthfulness will be questioned. For example, circumstances require you to be grief-stricken or worried, but corresponding changes don't occur in your body, voice or face. Your lie will be exposed. Every time you fail to emotionally, physically or verbally connect to what you say and do, you risk being caught in the lie.

> *When we make up the truth, it doesn't look or feel the same as it does in real life – we're guessing about the intensity and appearance of it.*

Deception in the Audition

"De-fictionalizing the fiction" is much easier to do if you have days, weeks or months to work on the material. However, if you get the material a day or even hours before the audition, the challenge of achieving deception will be much more difficult. It's like life – if we have time to formulate and tell a well-crafted lie, the odds of someone believing us are much greater than if we have to tell a complicated lie on the spot.

The moment you walk into the casting director's office for an audition, the deception begins. You may be nervous or possibly scared out of your wits, but you must conceal or control it in some way, or you'll appear unprofessional. Your body, voice and facial expressions cannot betray you. For example, if casting asks you how you're doing, you must quickly mask any fear you may have with a smile and respond, "Great!" That is your first act of deception – making sure they think you're confident, professional and in control, even if you're not.

To book the job, the most important deception comes into play. The stakes are very high. As you stand in front of the people who have the ability to hire you, you must turn the lies on the pages into truth. You must convince them that you are not an actor in their office, but a bloodthirsty drug lord in the middle of a drug buy, on a yacht off the hot and humid Florida coast. You must find a way to control or manage every impulse, twitch, action, or facial reaction that isn't in alignment with the truth you're trying to reveal, your character or the situation. If your deception is successful, you might just book the role. On the other hand, if any details fail to ring true, you'll be caught lying and forfeit the job.

Does this audition situation sound familiar to you? You walked into casting, you knew your lines and you knew your intentions. You worked with your acting coach for over an hour. So why didn't you get a callback or book the job? One answer is that you may have still been in a *lying state of mind* during the audition.

I want to draw a distinction between: a) someone saying you're lying because they didn't believe your action or what you were saying, and b) being in a lying state of mind.

When you have to remember what your intentions are, what you need to say, where you should look, how you should look and/or who you should look at – or you're not sure what you mean by what you say – then you're in a lying state of mind. In other words, you haven't supplied enough detail for your brain to accept the reality you're presenting to it.

The words you're saying are not yours; they're a fabrication, created by someone else. If you can't remember what they are, the meaning behind them or how you feel about what you're saying, you'll not only get caught in the lie, but pegged as a bad liar – and in this case, a bad actor. You have to create and often describe events that did not happen and do it with the appropriate opinion, feeling or emotion. Finally, to be believable, you must execute everything in a natural way that reflects real life. That's a very tall order for most.

As long as you are in a lying state of mind, you'll have a very difficult time as an on-camera actor achieving deception. Why more so for the on-camera actor? Because the camera creates more intimacy and brings more focus not only to the words spoken, but also to the three expressive nonverbal channels. It's these channels – your body, voice and face – by which the viewer will evaluate, determine and judge whether you're a truth teller or not. When you're in a lying state of mind, those three channels seem to have a mind of their own and will, with or without your awareness, expose your lie.

Deception on the Set

Unlike the audition where there's no set, props or actors to play off of (except for a reader – who is usually a *bad* liar), once you have the job the deception gets a bit easier. It's easier because you're often carrying out your deception on set or location. There are other actors to work with who are involved in the deception with you. You get time to memorize and understand your lines and their meaning. You can work out the intricacies of your character's thoughts and actions.

Although easier, it still has its challenges. The challenges come in when you have to manufacture the reality again from scratch. For example, you get cast in *Men in Black 8*. Your character is a hard-nosed fighter pilot and you're shooting a scene in a high-speed jet from the future, 30,000 feet in the air, in the middle of an alien invasion. At least that's what it will ultimately look like. But for now, you're in a tiny enclosed capsule, suspended 10 feet in the air, in front of a green screen. Any enemy spaceships or evil aliens you disintegrate must be fabricated through your imagination. Inches from you, a camera will be capturing every little nuance that appears on your face. You need to respond with the correct timing, emotional intensity and duration – with your body and voice, and most importantly your face – to cues given to you through your ear prompter. The success of your imaginary mission to avoid alien takeover will be dependent on how well you turn the lies into truth.

In his interviews, Will Smith talks about working in front of a green screen saying, "You *do* have to have a big imagination to work with visual effects." It goes without saying, using your imagination is mandatory. However, Will Smith is underselling his unquestionable ability to convince us that what he is seeing is real. Applying your imagination for the camera so that it picks up the appropriate subtleties of your thoughts, feelings and emotions the way Will Smith can is a whole different ballgame.

Because the camera is not selective in what it captures, to achieve deception you must be selective about what truth you reveal. You must:

- Know what the *truth* feels like in your body, sounds like in your voice and looks like on your face.
- Know what the *lie* feels like in your body, sounds like in your voice and looks like on your face.

- Have the skill to know the difference and the tools to make lies look like truth.

To be a believable, moving and successful on-camera actor, you need to raise the bar very high. You need to go way beyond playing make-believe and enter a very dangerous and exciting world where lies look like truth. And you need to understand the role that nonverbal communication plays in revealing that truth.

Now that we've explored lies and truth, and how we communicate both nonverbally, it's time to bring our focus to the role your face plays in achieving deception.

Chapter 3

Who's Getting All the On-Camera Work and Why?

Before we talk about who's getting all the on-camera work, let me ask you a personal question. Are you really prepared to be an on-camera actor? In my seminars, I often ask actors, "How many of you are really serious about your craft and want to be successful on-camera actors?" This is a no-brainer and 100% quickly raise their hands. Then I ask, "How many people have studied or are studying acting now?" Usually about 90% raise their hands. "How many have studied improv, movement, voice and diction?" The raised hands drop to about 75%. And then I ask, "How many people here have studied the nature and experience of emotions and what they look and feel like on your face from the most subtle to the extreme?" I look at the room and it's filled with guilty, bewildered faces, as if they somehow knew that they should have studied it but hadn't. All hands are down.

> *The most significant difference between stage and on-camera acting revolves around how your face reveals emotion.*

Stage Acting vs. On-Camera Acting

There are obvious differences between acting in these two environments. Stage has a continuous flow of action, whereas film is often shot out of sequence. Stage is done in one take; on-camera acting may involve dozens of takes. On stage, you must be heard by all. When acting on camera, a microphone will pick up your voice.

They also have similarities. Both involve hitting marks and finding your light. Both share understanding your character, objectives and relationships. So, what is the difference in acting?

Stage acting communicates emotion through your body, your voice and tone, as well as the words. On-camera acting needs something more intimate, something that can only be read in a medium or close-up shot. And that brings us back to your face.

Do you know how and what your face communicates?

Think about this. If you are a stage actor, you don't need to be as concerned with this skill for the simple reason that most often the audience can't see the subtleties of your face because they are too far away. If the audience wants to know what you're feeling, they'll have to pay attention to your voice and watch for physical movements, which need to be big enough for them to see. From the back row of the theater, the audience will be able to tell by the crackling or harshness of your voice and posturing of your body that you are getting emotional. However, if no words are spoken, they won't know what emotion you are feeling or the exact moment you begin to feel it. To do that, they would need to see your face. The face is the source by which we read what a person is feeling.

The facial reaction, subtle or otherwise, is exclusive to on-camera acting. Your whole audition for a TV show, film, commercial, or print job may depend on one emotional facial reaction.

The 5% Club

Statistics may vary from year to year, but my training and years of teaching have led me to certain beliefs about the craft of acting – especially on-camera acting. I know, as almost all acting teachers and coaches know, that only about 5% of the actors we teach have a real chance at success. This 5% has the talent to interpret material, make strong choices, execute their choices and take directorial adjustments. It would be great to be in that 5%, wouldn't it? But what about the rest?

The Promising 20%

Before you get all bummed out, I'm not saying that the remaining 95% of actors don't have any talent, because many of them do. Some have more talent than others, but talent isn't the only thing to consider when talking about one's success in acting. You have to include other factors like dedication, intelligence, perseverance, psychological issues, and timing, just to name a few. Out of that remaining 95%, I can safely say that 75% of those actors I've worked with over the past two decades had challenges in one of those areas mentioned. Meaning, 20% don't.

When you look carefully at this 20%, they're just as committed as the 5%. They understand the work and the process. In fact, many often make a living doing theater, but for one reason or another, they've been unable to cross over to on-camera acting.

I hear so often that a good actor can work both on stage and on-camera. But can they all? The truth is that not everyone is suited for the intimate venue of on-camera work. Think about it, when the talkies replaced silent films, many actors found themselves out of work. Their voice or speech patterns weren't suited for this new art form. The same is true for those who graduate from their training as skilled stage actors and look to transition to on-camera work.

But is the successful Broadway actor less talented because he can't seem to work on-camera? Or is an Academy nominated actor any less talented because they seem lost on a big stage? I think not. These are two different venues and different skills are needed to be successful at each.

So, the real questions are – what are the skills needed for on-camera work and how does one learn them?

Through my research into the science of emotion, I've come to understand that for the "promising 20%" of the acting population, there's a missing link which can be traced back to the actor, their training, or both. And what I've come to learn is that the majority of those actors have problems with either understanding, creating, or revealing emotions. Perhaps the 5% were born and raised to do it better?

If you are part of that 20%, your fate has not been sealed. There is now a way to level the playing field and gain the secrets of the 5% Club.

This book is dedicated to that relentlessly hardworking 20%

The Challenges of the 20%

If you're part of the 20% I'm referring to, you may have spent years working on your craft and building up an impressive resume of stage credits and awards, but you're feeling stalled and frustrated when it comes to TV, film, or commercial auditions. You probably find it difficult to translate or adjust what you've learned about stage acting for use in front of the camera. That may even include a still camera – when having headshots taken.

You might be saying things like:

- "I'm often told that my acting is too big or too small."
- "When I'm in a scene or commercial audition, I'm constantly told to make it real. I think I'm real, but apparently I'm not."
- "Most of my headshots looks the same."
- "When I see myself on the screen, I can tell I'm not revealing what I'm feeling."
- "It seems like no one knows what I'm feeling."
- "I have a difficult time identifying the various levels of emotion in scenes – and revealing those emotions on my face."
- "I can't seem to stop my face from moving."
- "I feel more comfortable on stage than I do in front of the camera."
- "When I'm asked to give a specific reaction or emotional reveal, I'm often confused or feel that I fail at my attempts."

These are just some of the obstacles that many actors come across when they're trying to make the transition from stage to on-camera acting. If not resolved, these obstacles can put you at a serious disadvantage. You may have been told that "acting is acting," "you just need to adjust it for the camera," "you're just not doing the craft correctly," or that "you need to focus more on the circumstances, be more honest, develop your imagination and commit." Well, that might explain what you're doing wrong, but it doesn't explain what the 5% does right.

The 5% Secret

The challenge of emotional reveals became even clearer to me when I got into commercial casting. I started to notice that the problem of coming up with and revealing specific reactions wasn't unique to me. In fact, from what I witnessed, the vast majority of actors were in the same predicament.

Countless actors came in to audition looking lost or confused when I asked them to react to something they were seeing, touching, tasting, hearing, or thinking. The problem was even more pronounced if the reaction had to be based on something supplied by their imagination. Yet, there were some actors who were really good at it – and I noticed that those actors were getting the callbacks. And it was a select few who were consistently booking the jobs. If you haven't guessed by now, they were part of the 5%.

The 6 Things that the 5% Does Differently

Since these actors were good at this type of audition, I wanted to know what they were doing that set them apart from the rest, so I studied them. As time went by, I noticed that they all did 6 things that helped them land the job. The reaction(s) they came up with were:

- Real
- Recognizable
- Appropriate and Adjustable
- Revealed one at a time (isolate)
- Repeatable
- On demand

Let's look at these six things in detail to see just why these actors stood out from the others.

Real

All the top actors I studied had the ability to make their reactions real. "Making it real" is important in every aspect of an on-camera actor's work. If you don't have the skill to make what you're doing or reacting to read as real and believable, it simply won't work.

You can't pretend to be reacting to something – you have to do it with enough detail that it looks like real life. The reactions of the 5% came out of something they were really thinking, seeing, touching, tasting, hearing, or smelling. It was either physical or created by their imagination.

To get the callback and ultimately book the job, you must be skilled at executing the action as well as the reaction. In other words, you are doing something (the action) and then something happens that you respond to (the reaction) in a very real way.

Recognizable

The group of actors who got callbacks and booked the jobs created specific thoughts, feelings and emotions and manifested what they were thinking or feeling on their faces in a way that was recognizable. For example, they were able to create and reveal thoughts and feelings such as disappointment, surprise, awe, confusion, or disbelief. Other actors may have had the same thoughts or feelings, but either those emotions never reached their faces or they were unrecognizable.

Why wouldn't your expression be recognizable? Many actors are taught to be open and respond to what is happening in the moment. This style of acting gives the actor freedom and appears to give their work more life. In researching emotions, what I found to be quite interesting was that your face has 43 muscles and over 10,000 different expressions it can make. About 8,000 of those expressions are related to emotions. The rest have no emotional meaning at all. They are just facial movements. Out of 10,000 different possible expressions, the 5% actors chose the ones that had meaning.

The actors I was studying didn't seem to have any more special training than the others. Some had improv experience, some didn't. Some had credits and acting training, some had no credits and very little acting training at all.

Appropriate and Adjustable

The third thing I noticed that the 5% did was to make their expression appropriate. By appropriate, I mean that the reaction they created was based on what was happening in the material or a direction that was given. It also made sense and had the proper intensity. If your reaction is random or the intensity is too big or small, it won't make sense to the viewer and will seem inappropriate for what's taking place.

The 5% actors could interpret the material or direction in a way that made their reaction appropriate – and if it was too big or too small, they could adjust it. Some actors stumbled upon the correct reaction, but they weren't able to adjust it appropriately.

One Reaction at a Time (Isolate)

The group I studied didn't have multiple facial movements. There was <u>one</u> recognizable, appropriate facial reaction at a time.

Most often, an actor will try to create a reaction by recalling a time that they felt something analogous to the circumstances, then hope that the correct reaction will appear on their face. As they do this, other thoughts cross their mind and those additional thoughts are also reflected on their face. Sometimes those thoughts are accompanied by body movement. So, even if the correct reaction is given, the extraneous movement of the face and body often makes the reaction too big, too busy, or unrecognizable. The actors who were booking were able to isolate the appropriate response and moved from one clear, recognizable, appropriate reaction to the next.

Repeatable

I also noticed that the 5% actors could repeat the reaction they gave. I discovered that this was because they were very in tune to what their faces were saying. The actors who had this ability were in alignment with what they were feeling and what they were revealing, making them more capable of repeating exactly what they did. So if you can't repeat what worked, odds are you aren't going to book the job, and if you do happen to book, there's a chance you could lose it by not being able to repeat on set what you did in the audition.

On Demand

Finally, what the 5% actors were able to do was interpret material, make a choice, express that choice in a real, recognizable and appropriate way – and do it when asked. In other words, they were able to do it on demand. If they got an adjustment, they understood and executed it without losing any intensity or meaning to what they had done prior.

Many actors, if given enough time and guidance, can come up with the same result. However, time is not often on your side in the audition setting and guidance may be very limited. Somehow the actors who booked the job (notice now I'm saying, "booked the job," not just "got a callback") intuitively knew how to interpret and execute their choices. They had the skill to adjust when needed and did so without much effort.

Think about it for moment. If you don't know what you did and/or don't know how you did it, how can you make the adjustment? If you can't give them what they want, the way they want it, when they want it, how can you expect them to hire you?

Putting it All Together

What separates the 5% from the 20% is that the 5% can consistently come up with real, recognizable, appropriate, and repeatable emotional facial reactions and do it on demand. The fact that these actors were able to repeat what most couldn't even create meant there was some conscious or unconscious skill involved that was directly related to on-camera acting. The 5% did this naturally. No one taught them this specific aspect of acting. And because they did it naturally, they appeared to be more skilled than others.

> *It became evident to me that facial reactions were a required part of on-camera acting... I just didn't realize how much.*

Understanding what the 5% were doing not only defined what made them stand out from the rest, but also defined the difference between stage and on-camera acting.

Misconceptions of How the 5% Do What They Do

I've conducted thousands of interviews with actors, acting teachers, directors, casting directors, and photographers. Most believe that what makes the 5% more skilled than others is that they can adjust their stage acting training for the camera by doing one or more of the following:

- *Making everything smaller* – Because the camera picks up and magnifies information, actors are told to minimize all verbal and physical actions/reactions. While there are certainly situations in which a more subtle (smaller) reaction is appropriate, the blanket statement of "make *everything* smaller" does not universally work.

- *Bringing their emotions through their eyes* – The eyes can communicate many things, but the eyes alone are not enough to fully create most emotions. Yet, actors are often told to keep the body still and allow only the eyes to communicate their thoughts, feelings, and emotions.

- *Real thinking* – There are those who believe that all an actor has to do is to have a thought and the camera will pick it up. This is only true for a small percentage of actors who are able to accurately reveal their thoughts through their facial expressions. For so many others, thoughts *don't* register on their faces. Is it interesting to watch someone think if they don't reveal <u>what</u> they're thinking? I think not.

- *Being honest* – The belief here is that if you truthfully and honestly create what you want to reveal or hide from others, it will appear on your face appropriately. Some actors are able to do this, but most are not because again, for a variety of reasons, they're not showing what they're creating.

For the 5% of the actors and those who view, direct, and teach them, these adjustments seem to explain why they are successful on-camera actors. In fact, there are many classes that specifically teach and promote these practices. Again, this may *look* like what the 5% is doing right, but it isn't necessarily so. And if you're part of the 20%, these adjustments may offer absolutely NO HELP, as well as leave you completely frustrated. If that is the case for you, it may not be error on your part. You just may need to dig a little deeper. We'll discuss each of these beliefs in more detail in chapter 6.

Understanding what the 5% does explains what you are really looking at when you turn the sound off and just watch the actors' faces. You are reading real, recognizable, appropriate, emotional facial reactions. Let's take a look at what science knows about emotions and how it applies to on-camera acting.

Most importantly, let's dig in and uncover what the 5% are doing and how you can achieve it.

Chapter 4

The Secret Language Your Face Speaks

What's been missing in your on-camera training may have been staring you in the face all along.

After working with thousands of actors and studying the work of leading researchers in the field of emotions, I discovered that the face speaks a very specific, cognitive, emotional, and emblematic language. I learned that there are universal emotions that people will recognize anywhere on the planet.

These universal emotions also have precise muscle groups or muscle patterns that are distinct to each of these emotions. Within these universal emotions are families of other emotions that are all related and share the same muscle groups. When an emotion or a strong, opinionated thought occurs, subtle changes in the face appear.

The creating and revealing of these real, recognizable, appropriate, emotional facial expressions is what I call "The Language of the Face." To be more specific, this language is a method of human nonverbal communication that uses specific facial muscle movements at various intensities and speed to communicate thoughts, feelings and emotions.

Charles Darwin was one of the first to recognize that the face spoke a specific, recognizable language. In his book, *The Expression of Emotions in Man and Animals*, published in 1872, Darwin discussed the universal nature of facial expressions and the muscle groups used to express them. Darwin's work wasn't widely well received at the time. The thoughts of the day were that emotions were culturally learned and not universal. In other words, every culture had their own way of expressing emotions. This thinking lasted for almost 100 years.

The 7 Universal Emotions

In the late 1960's, Dr. Paul Ekman came on to the scene. Ekman's research into emotions and their relation to facial expressions renewed Darwin's theories and took his work to a whole new level. Studying a remote tribe in the highlands of Papua, New Guinea, Ekman discovered that these tribesmen, who were never exposed to the outside world, not only expressed surprise, fear, anger, disgust, sadness, and happiness with the same muscle groups and patterns, but for the same reasons as the rest of the world. This study revealed that these six emotions were biological in origin and universal across all cultures. Contempt later became the seventh emotion to be added to the list.

#1

7 Universal Emotions

SURPRISE | FEAR | DISGUST | CONTEMPT

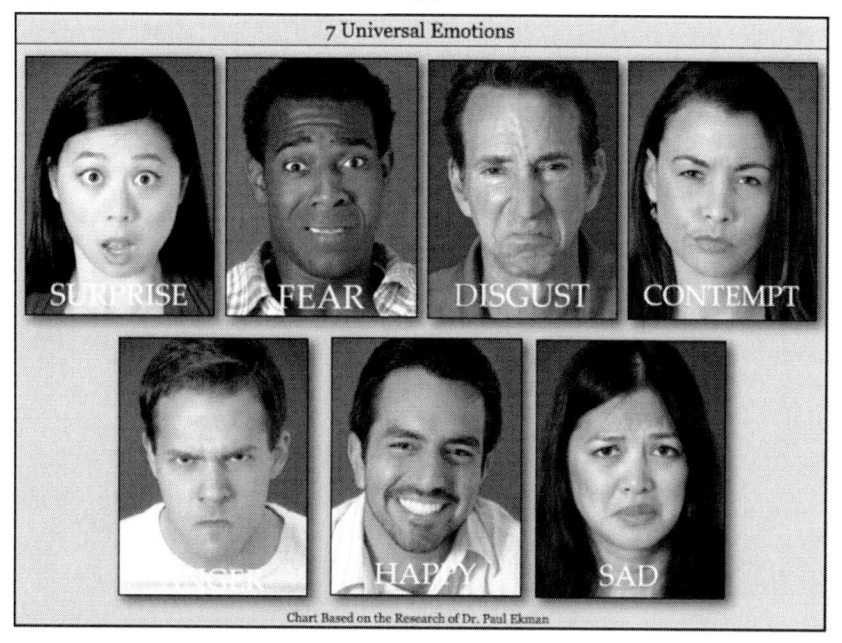

ANGER | HAPPY | SAD

Chart Based on the Research of Dr. Paul Ekman

Why Should You Study Emotions?

Because as an actor, you're in the emotional communications business. Understanding, creating and revealing emotions is critical to your on-camera acting success. Yet very few actors know about emotions or what they look like – not just when they are fully expressed, but the subtleties of the emotion when it's just beginning or trying to be managed.

- If you don't know about the nature and experience of emotions, how can you truly interpret all the emotions the character is feeling and why they are feeling them?

- If you don't know what the character is feeling, how do you know what reaction is appropriate to give?

- If you don't know the sensations and impulses produced by the emotions when you create them, how do

- you know where you are in the experience of the emotion?
- Most importantly for the on-camera actor, if you don't know what these emotions look and feel like on your face, how will you know you are truthfully communicating them?

Your face and what it expresses influences the person looking at it. And it's vital to every part of the actor's journey from headshot to close-up.

Universality of Emotions and Acting

How often have you heard that casting directors and directors "know it when they see it?" They *know* it because they can *recognize* it.

The recognition of these unique facial muscles when someone becomes emotional is responsible for your understanding of the Language of the Face. Without a word spoken, we're able to pick up facial cues from others that tell us if they are upset, frightened, confused, or feeling happy. The same is true in film and television, where we can see what the actor is feeling or thinking just by "reading" his or her face. Although it can be quite subtle, we can identify the moment when an actor becomes emotional simply by the recognition of one or more of the emotional facial muscle groups appearing or leaving his or her face.

Think of the 7 universal emotions in the same way you think of the 3 primary colors. By blending these 3 primary colors in different combination and amounts, you can come up with an infinite amount of colors. The same is true for the 7 emotions. As you understand the Language of the Face, you will begin to comprehend. Every recognizable emotional facial reaction is part of one of the muscle groups of the 7 universal emotions, a combination of muscle groups, or a blend of one or more of the muscle groups. What was on the face of the 5% actors was recognizable.

The more muscle groups applied to each of the universal emotions or the more tension, contraction, or expansion you give to the muscle group, the bigger and more intense the expression. Conversely, when you take away muscle groups, tension, expansion, or contraction, the smaller the expression. This is how the 5% made their reaction appropriate and adjustable.

When we look at the things that the 5% did to book the job – creating recognizable, appropriate, adjustable, repeatable, and real reactions, one at a time, we can clearly see that they were speaking the Language of the Face.

How Your Face Speaks

This facial language is like any other language you learn to speak, it has rules and consequences for breaking those rules. If you use words arbitrarily, speak them out of context, use them with the wrong inflection, intonation, at best, people will miss your intended message. At worse, you risk being perceived as confusing, untruthful or dishonest.

On the other hand, having the skill to speak this facial language clearly and authentically not only makes you a more effective, dynamic and charismatic communicator, but in the world of acting, it's what will define you as an on-camera storyteller.

To understand the language that your face speaks and why it speaks the way it does, you have to understand what emotions are, what makes you or your character emotional, and the ways you/he/she reveals emotion. Knowing when and why we become emotional, as well as how much we will reveal of what we feel, will give you greater insight into understanding your character, as well as yourself.

What are Emotions and When do we Get Emotional?

Simply put, emotions are *reactions* to matters that seem very important to our welfare. When acting on camera, in order to know whether or not you should react to something, you need to know if it matters to your character.

   According to Dr. Ekman and other leading researchers, the most common way an emotion occurs is when you sense that something important is happening, or is about to happen, that will have a positive or negative impact on you. What you sense may be real or imaginary. It may be happening now, or you sense that it will happen in the future.

   Emotions can also occur in other ways such as remembering a past emotional event, talking about a past emotional event, or through empathy or violation of social norms. Believe it or not, you can also become emotional by simply assuming the appearance of an emotion. When we use the muscle group to create what an emotion looks like on our face, we often start to feel that emotion. Whatever the reason we become emotional, the result is the same – we feel differently, think differently, and act differently.

Universal Triggers, Sensations and Impulses

Dr. Ekman didn't limit his work to muscle groups. His research also concluded that each of the 7 universal emotions had unique and universal triggers, sensations, and impulses.

While we all don't get emotional about the same things, the *result of what we get emotional about* can all be traced back to the universal themes. For example, getting fired from your job or having a good friend reject you. Either of these events can make you sad if you perceive them as a meaningful loss. Once an emotion is triggered, the brain prepares the body to take action.

This preparation for action is what stimulates the universal sensations. For example, if something triggers anger in you, you'll begin to feel the sensations of that emotion. Your temperature will begin to rise, your heart will start beating faster, and you'll feel warmth in your arms and hands. These changes in your body are preparing and compelling you to deal with or remove the cause of the anger.

If you have no awareness or need to manage/hide what you're feeling, the facial muscles associated with anger that appear on your face will be a warning to whoever sees them. You're about to get aggressive in some way.

Take Notice

Next time you feel irritated or annoyed with someone, notice any changes that may be occurring in your body.

You may begin to feel slight muscle tension around the ridge of your lips, tension in your eyelids or a slight pulling down of your brow.

Your breathing and heart rate may quicken, even if just for a moment. You may feel a slight contraction in your muscles or a tingling sensation on the back of your neck.

You might feel a little change in your overall body temperature.

These signals will increase the more irritated or annoyed you get.

You're on your way to anger!

Understanding emotional triggers helps to guide your interpretation of what's happening. The emotional trigger is *why* your face is speaking to us in the first place. It's your motivation. The sensations give you the physical clues as to where you are in the experience of the emotion. The impulses are the actions you are impelled to take.

Following are the 7 biological, universal emotions along with a brief overview of their muscle groups, triggers, sensations, and impulses.

#2

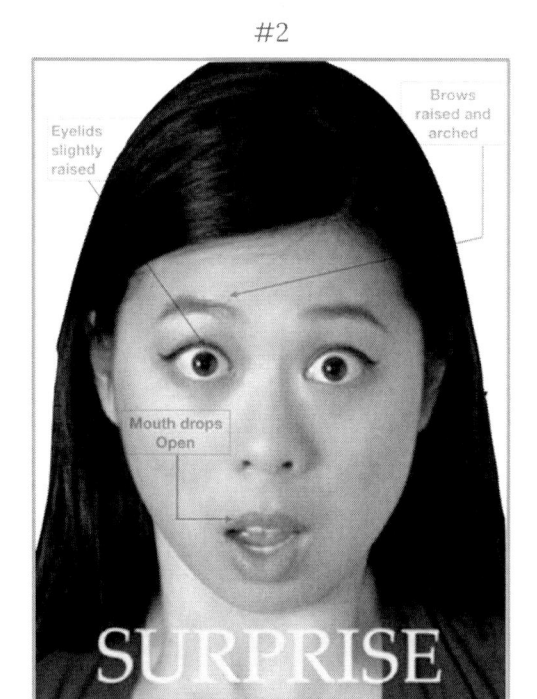

Eyelids slightly raised
Brows raised and arched
Mouth drops Open

SURPRISE

(Photo #2) Surprise uses three muscle groups: the brows are raised, the eyelids are raised, and the mouth drops open in a relaxed manner.

Surprise has a fairly large family. Within it, you'll find awe, wonderment, amazement, being dumbfounded, questioning, and doubt, to name a few. It's a neutral emotion, meaning it's neither positive nor negative. It's the briefest of all the emotions because this expression doesn't stay on your face long before it is followed by another expression that shows your evaluation of the surprising event.

- **Triggers**: Something sudden, unexpected, or novel.
- **Sensation**: A moment of disorientation or uneasiness.
- **Impulse**: To orient or obtain more information.

#3

Brows slightly raised drawn together

The upper eyelid is raised above the iris and the bottom lid is tensed.

Lips are either tensed slightly and/or pulled back.

FEAR

(Photo #3) Fear uses 3 muscle groups: the brows are raised and drawn together, the upper eyelids are raised/the lower eyelids are tensed, and the lips are tensed/stretched back or down.

Although fear and surprise share the same muscle groups, if you compare them, you can clearly see the difference. Surprise is brief and there's no tension in any of the muscle groups. In the fear family you will also find worry, apprehension, horror, and terror.

- **Triggers:** Threat to physical or psychological well-being.
- **Sensations:** The breath quickens and the heart beats faster. Warm sensations are felt in the legs. It's hard to swallow.
- **Impulses:** To run away, freeze, avoid, or minimize the threat.

#4

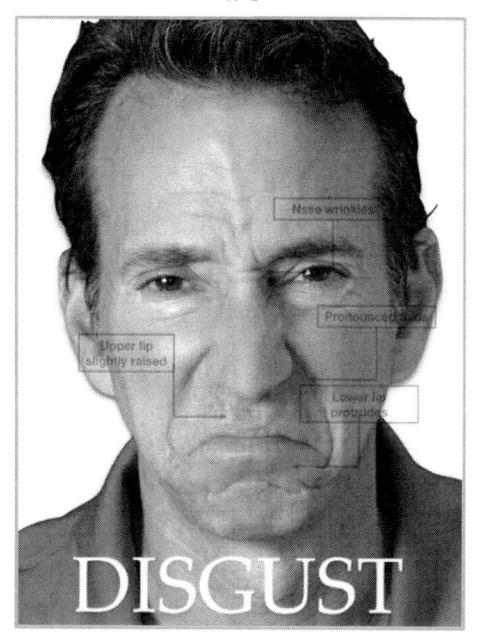

DISGUST

(Photo #4) Disgust can be expressed in two areas. The upper lip raises toward the nose or the nose wrinkles. When both muscle groups come into play, the cheeks rise, and the brow pulls down.

In the disgust family you'll find everything from dislike, distaste, disapproval, and revulsion.

- **Triggers**: Contamination, something offensive, rotten objects.
- **Sensations**: Mild tension in the stomach to wrenching, gagging, and vomiting.
- **Impulses**: Aversion, elimination of the contaminated object or thought.

#5

CONTEMPT

(**Photo #5**) **Contempt**: Tightening and lifting of the lip corner on one side of the mouth.

Contempt is the only emotion that is asymmetrical and moves laterally. If you're judging someone or their actions to be stupid or below you, you're more than likely experiencing contempt. Contempt can also be a fun emotion to experience, like when you're feeling a little cocky, or thinking you're above someone or superior.

- **Triggers**: Immoral action, a feeling of intellectual superiority.
- **Sensations**: Will vary depending on the trigger.
- **Impulses**: To assert superiority.

#6

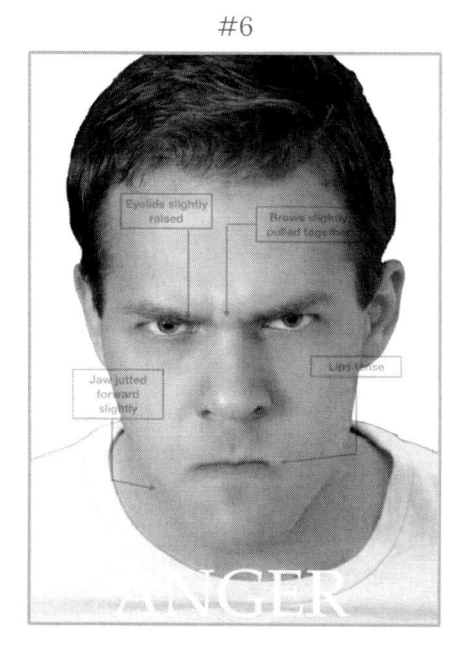

(Photo #6) **Anger** uses 3 muscle groups: the brows are pulled down and together, the upper eyelids are raised/lower eyelids are tense, and the lips are tightened. Anger is a very complex emotion and has a big family. Parts of this emotion appear when we are thinking, confused, or perplexed. They also appear when we are determined to do something. Other emotions you will find in anger are annoyance, irritation, frustration, and rage.

- **Triggers:** Goal obstruction, injustice, perceived violation of society norms, disappointments, someone else's anger, self-preservation.

- **Sensations:** Heart and breath speed up. You may feel slight tension in your jaw, warmth in your hands, and/or the hair on the back of your neck stands up.

- **Impulses:** Remove the obstacle. To control, punish, or retaliate.

#7

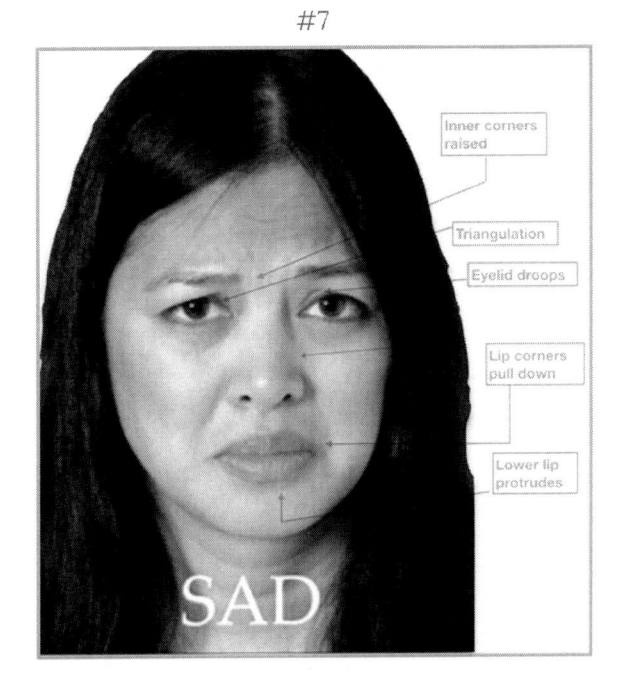

[Photo of woman's face labeled "SAD" with annotations: Inner corners raised, Triangulation, Eyelid droops, Lip corners pull down, Lower lip protrudes]

(**Photo #7**) ***Sadness*** uses 2 muscle groups: the inner corners of the brows are raised, the eyelids droop, and there is a downturn of the lip corners.

The sad family includes helplessness, hopelessness, disappointment, and longing, to name a few. For the actor, sadness can be a black hole you will sink into because when you are sad for a while, you no longer have any impulses. You don't want anything.

- **Triggers:** Any meaningful loss.
- **Sensations:** Overwhelming sense of heaviness in the body. It might even be difficult to swallow.
- **Impulses:** Recouping the loss or none.

#8

Wrinkles form below the eye and corners.

raised cheeks

Corners are drawn back and up.

HAPPY

(Photo #8) Happiness: Raised lip corners and cheeks, crow's feet wrinkles, and narrowing of the eyes.

Happy covers all the positive emotions from sensory pleasures, amusement, and contentment to pride in accomplishment. It's the most recognized of all the emotions. We smile for many reasons. We smile to break the ice upon meeting someone new, to seem more agreeable or submissive. However, there is a difference between a cordial smile and a genuine smile of happiness.

- **Triggers**: Goal attainment, accomplishment, pleasure, or excitement.
- **Sensations**: Overall sense of well-being.
- **Impulses**: To seek more experiences.

The Way Emotions Appear on Your Face

The 7 universal emotions appear on your face in different ways for different reasons. The three main ways emotions appear on your face are macro, micro, and subtle.

- **Macro Expression:** This is a full intensity emotional facial expression that appears when there is no need to manage or hide the emotion in any way. Macro expressions last longer and are more emotionally intense than other kinds of expressions. Macro expressions often involve the whole face and are expressed with all the muscle groups. The above photos of the 7 Universal Emotions are macro expressions.

- **Micro Expression:** This is a full expression of an emotion that for one reason or another is trying to be concealed. Micro expressions are very quick – usually less than half a second. Recognition of what emotion was expressed is typically missed by the average person, yet you can instinctively tell *something* has happened.

  Micro expressions can also be seen as "emotional leakage." Executed correctly, these expressions can give insight to what your character is feeling, but for whatever reason, is trying to conceal. For example, if you were trying to conceal your anger, you may see leakage of it flashing from the mouth, brows, or eyes.

- **Subtle Expression:** Unlike macro expressions, subtle expressions are lower intensity and occur when a person is just starting to feel an emotion, when the emotional response is of lower intensity, or when someone is trying to manage or cover up a full emotion but is not entirely able to do so. The same muscle groups in the macro expressions of the emotion will be involved, but they'll be expressed with less contraction, expansion, or tension.

Emotions that involve multiple muscle groups, when expressed as subtle, may only involve just parts of those muscle groups. For example, anger involves the brows, eyes, and mouth. The subtle expression may only involve the brows and the eyes, or just the mouth. These expressions are also known as *partial expressions*.

A Closer Look at Subtle Expressions

As you look at the individual faces in photo #9, can you see the hint of emotion on my face? Try this. For each photo, see if you can come up with a short explanation as to why I may look the way I do.

After the group photo, I'll compare the individual subtle photos to the corresponding macro, which will explain each of the expressions. See if it matches with your explanation.

#9

At the far left (photo #9) is my "static" shot, which means that I am looking as neutral as I possibly can. As you can see, there is a slight drooping of the upper eyelids, making my static look appear slightly sad.

Looking at the second photo from the left, you may have thought I was seeing something amazing or I was dumbfounded by something. In either case you would be right. It's subtle awe, which is in the surprise family. When you compare the macro to the subtle in photo #10, you see my eyelids are slightly raised and my mouth is slightly parted.

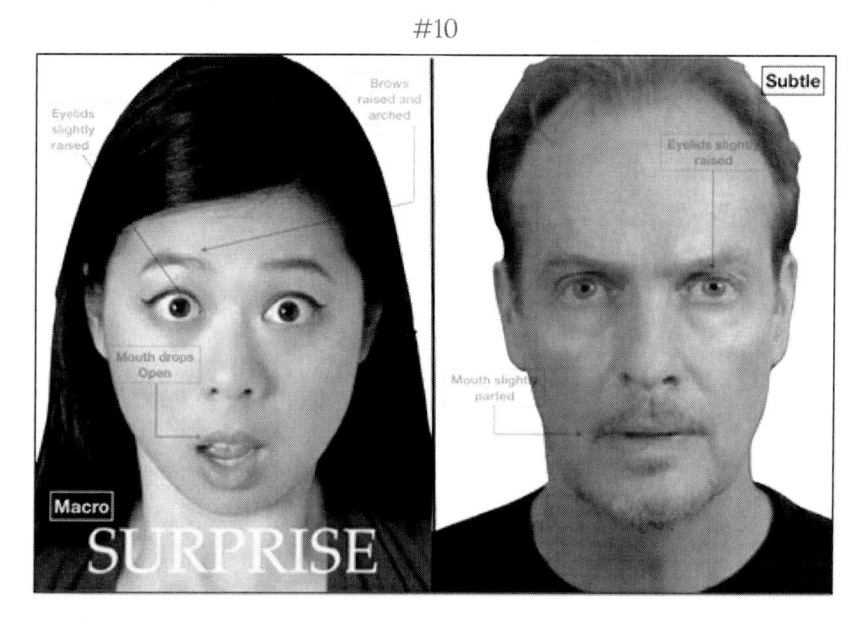

#10

The third image from the left (photo #9) is pretty obvious – slight happiness. If you look closely and compare the macro to the subtle in photo #11, you'll see the corners of my lips and cheeks are slightly raised and there is slight tension around my eyes.

#11

Subtle
Wrinkles form below the eye and corners
raised cheeks
Slight raised cheeks
Slight raised lip corners
HAPPY

If you guessed sadness for the photo on the far right (Photo #9), you're correct. When you compare the macro to the subtle in photo #12, you can see the lifting of the inner corners of my brows and the slight downturn of the corners of my lips.

#12

Subtle
Inner corners raised
Triangulation
Lip corners pull down
Lower lip protrudes
Macro
SAD

Check out this next set of subtle expressions (photo #13) and again try to come up with a short explanation as to why I may look the way I do in the shot.

#13

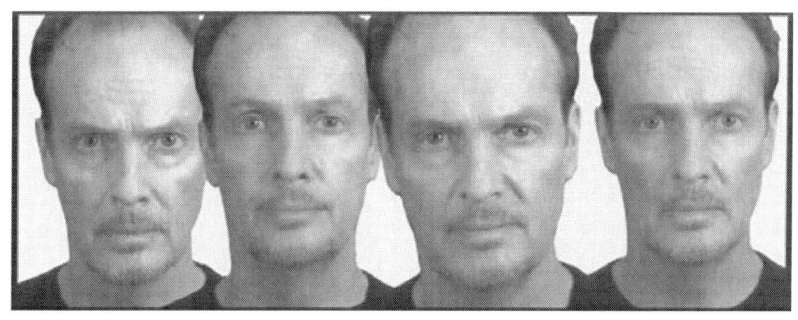

Starting with the photo at the far left (photo #13), if you compare the macro to the subtle (see photo #14) you'll see my brows are slightly pulled together and drawn down, and my eyelids are raised creating a harder stare. If you guessed anger for this photo, you are correct.

#14

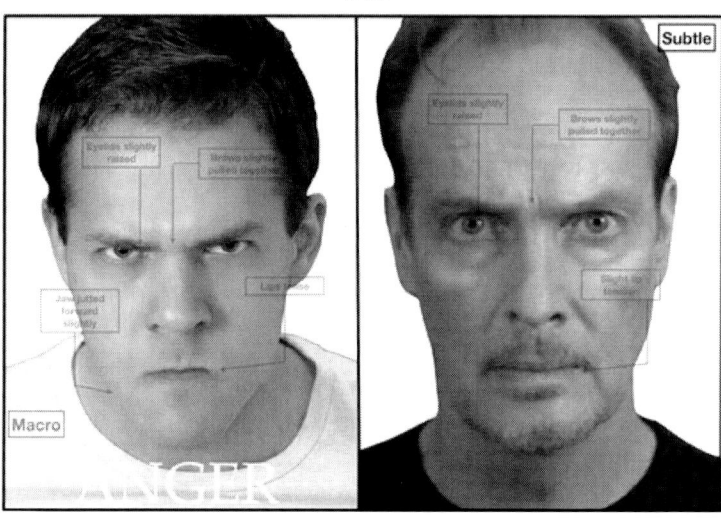

The second photo to the left (Photo #13) has a smugness to it. That's contempt. If you compare the macro to the subtle (see photo #15) you can see this by the slight tightening and lifting on one side of my mouth. There's definitely some judgment going on.

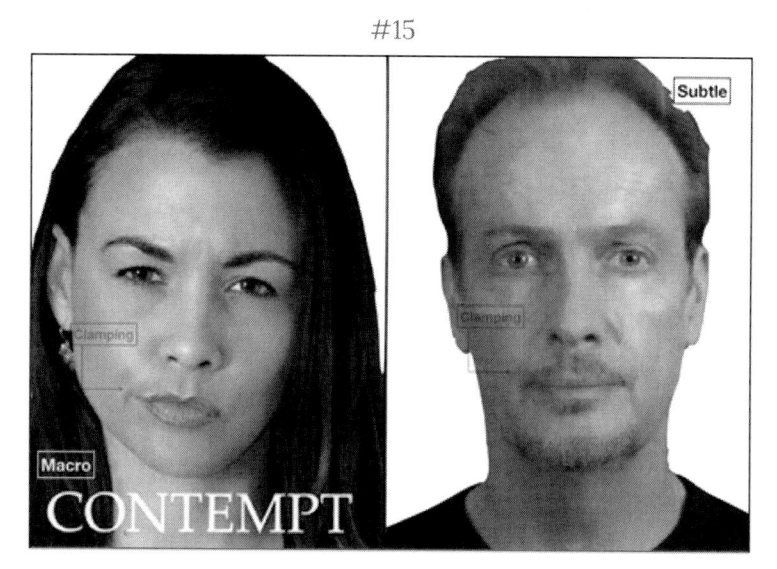

#15

CONTEMPT

You might not have been able to guess the photo third (Photo #13) from the left, but I would venture to say that you wouldn't like it if someone looked at you this way. As you compare the macro to the subtle (see photo #16) although very slight, my upper lip is lifting up towards my nose. You can tell by the two folds on each side of my nose. You might think it's distaste, disdain, or subtle disgust and you'd be correct.

#16

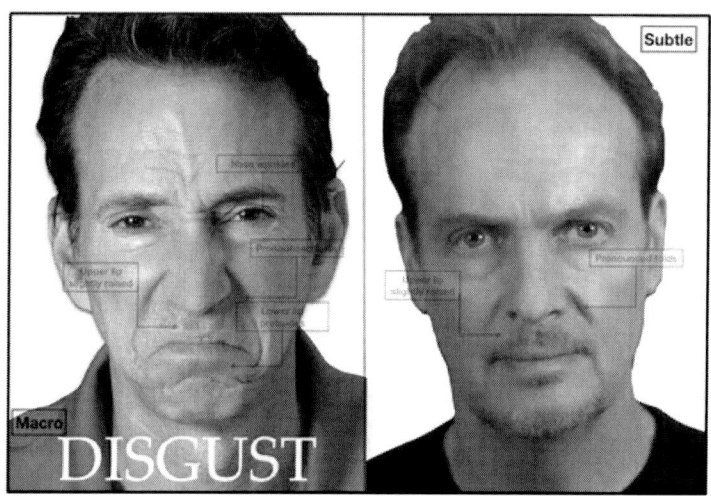

DISGUST — Macro | Subtle

If I look worried to you in the photo on the far right (photo #13), then you're correct. You may have thought I was sad because of my static eyelids. But look at my eyebrows. They're slightly lifted and drawn together, which indicates worry. Compare my subtle to the macro in photo #17 and see what you think.

#17

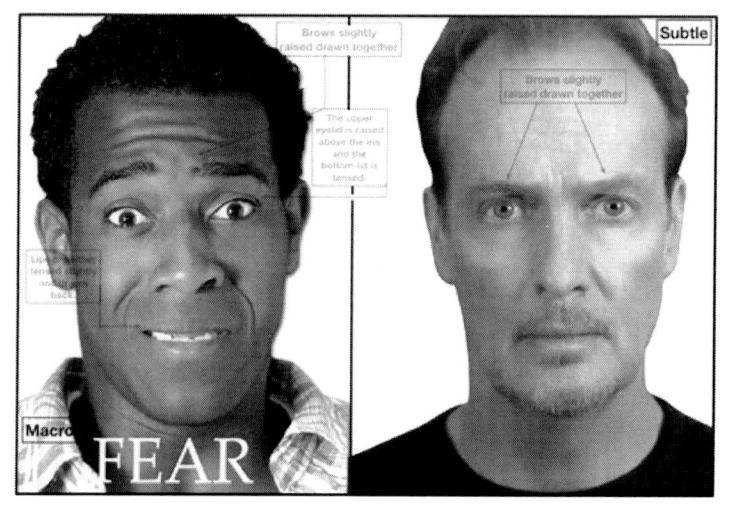

FEAR — Macro | Subtle

60

The Way Emotions Feel in Your Body

It's time to begin work with the different emotions. Refer to the photos and details about the 7 universal emotions that we just covered. Choose an emotion you want to work with, and see if you can activate one or more of the muscle groups within that emotion. As you work on each one, you'll see that not only does the appearance of your face change when you activate just one of the muscle groups, but you'll also begin to feel different. Try each one and notice how you feel. Here's an example of working with the emotion of Anger.

Anger Exercise

1. Slightly tense the muscles in your jaw as you jut it out slightly.
2. Your lower teeth may be even with the upper or slightly out further.
3. Move your jaw out until you begin to sense a little negative energy building.
4. Once you feel that energy building, press your teeth together. At this point, the negative energy should be growing.
5. To intensify the feeling even more, tense your lips as you press them together firmly. Don't pucker them, just press.
6. Be aware of any sensations that may be occurring.

Use the photos below (photo#18) to guide you. First photo is static. In the middle photo, the jaw is jutting forward. And on the far right, the teeth and lips are pressed together firmly.

#18

You know that you did this exercise correctly if you began to feel slightly irritated, annoyed or impatient. You may have noticed that your foot started tapping or twitching, or that your stare became fixed. Many people also notice that their heart rate and breathing started to increase.

How did you feel? Do it again and this time look in the mirror once you start to experience the change in yourself. Notice how little energy you're using to experience this change. Just by activating one muscle group in the anger family, you should see that not only has your whole face changed, but you've also begun to change emotionally.

Facial Volume and Speed

Think of the micro as the speed in which the face speaks. The micro is very fast. You can think of the macro and subtle expressions as the volume the face speaks. The macro tends to yell at you, while the subtle tends to whisper. At the same time, they can both convey a strong meaning, depending on the tension, contraction, or expansion of the muscle groups. When you're at an audition and you're asked for a bigger reaction, what they are looking for is a macro expression. When they want something smaller or what many think of as "real," they're talking about the subtle expression.

#19

The Genuine Smile

Look at the photos in #19. Although both are smiling, only one is a genuinely happy smile. Can you tell which one?

As I said earlier, we smile for many reasons, mostly social. Both smiles involve the smiling muscle (zygomaticus major), which raises the corners of the lips. The genuine smile on the right also involves the muscle surrounding the eye (orbicularis oculi). This smile is known as the Duchenne Smile, named after the French neurologist.

When we are experiencing a genuinely happy feeling, the orbicularis oculi contracts. There are two parts to this muscle. The inner part of the muscle tightens the eyelids and the skin directly below the eyes. The contracting of that muscle gives you the squinting look you see in the picture on the right.

The outer part of the genuine smile, which runs all around the eye socket, pulls down the eyebrows and the skin below the eyebrows, while at the same time pulling up the skin below the eyes and raising the cheeks (See photo #20).

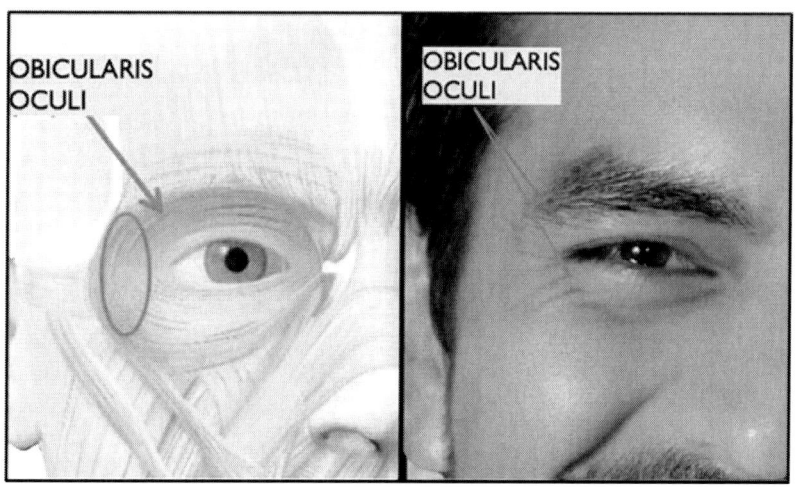

#20

Working on the inner part of the muscle, the eyelid tightener, is easy to do. The outer part, which contracts the muscle around the eye socket, is a different story. Only a small percentage of the population can activate this muscle without a genuinely happy feeling.

#21

It's incredibly hard to fake a genuinely happy smile. Take a look at Hillary Clinton's famous 'fake smile' (photo #21). She looks attractive and pleasant, but stiff and posing. Does your smiling headshot look like hers? If so, I strongly suggest taking a new one.

It's even harder to generate a genuine smile under any type of stress or through negative feelings. However, learning how to create it is your ticket to a successful smiling headshot. It's the engagement of this muscle that makes your smiling headshot pop, look genuine, and puts the sparkle in your eyes.

Other Ways Your Face Speaks the Language

Not all recognizable facial expressions are emotional. Some are cognitive or emblematic.

Cognitive refers to thinking. Some thinking doesn't take a lot of energy – it just causes us to slow down or stop what we're doing in order to solve a problem, or to simply daydream. But when the problem is more difficult or perplexing, we need focus. If that's the case, believe it or not, we often turn to the anger family. For example, the brows may pull in and down or there may be more tension in the eyes as you focus in on something. Or you may press your lips together or jut your jaw out slightly (see photo #22 left side). This is why a lot of people look angry when all they are doing is thinking.

Depending on what you're thinking about, this cognitive expression might blend with an emotion. Let's say you're worried about something and determined to find an answer. You'll likely be blending one of the muscle groups of fear with one of the muscle groups of anger.

#22

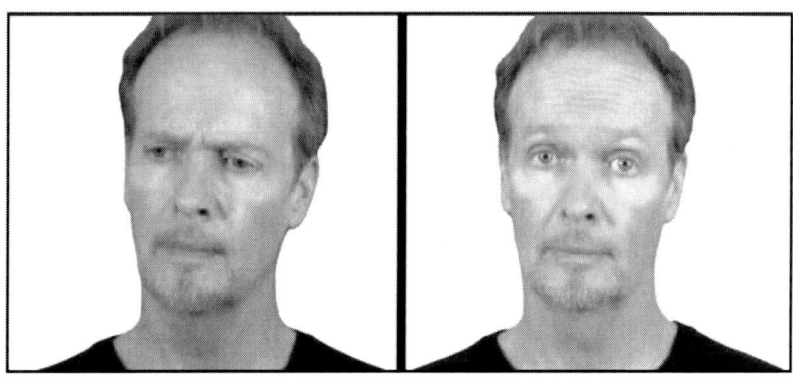

Emblems, on the other hand, are symbols that are culturally recognized. For example, saying everything is okay by giving a 'thumbs up.' Or saying everything is *not* okay by giving someone the middle finger. When you lift your brows up and hold them in that position, it is an emblem for questioning (see photo #22 right side). If the head tilts down slightly, it can read like doubt or slight skepticism. We use our eyebrows to communicate a lot. They can be a sign that you're alert and open – or even just a way of saying hello.

There are also *emotional emblems*. They look like the facial expression of the emotion, but are different enough for the viewer to know that you are not really feeling what you are showing. It's like feigning or mocking someone's anger with a sad expression or warning them that you will get angry if they overstep a boundary (see photo #23).

#23

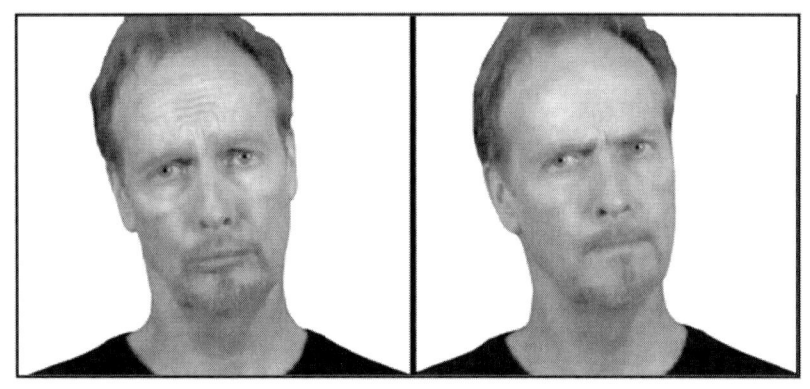

You might also let someone know how you feel or how you're going to feel. For example, you're telling a friend that you have to go see your accountant about taxes, then right after you tell him, you tense your lips and stretch your lips back and down. The person you're talking to will recognize the emotional symbol and knows that fear is coming from what will happen, not what you are feeling at that moment.

We also use our face to *punctuate* our words in the same way we might use our hands. Some people bring focus to a point they're making or just accent something with a raising of the brows or a widening of the eyes.

Unlike emblems, these facial movements are there to comment on what you're saying. They add a question mark, exclamation point, quotes, or period to our speech. For example, you might say, "It was really big," and as you say this, your eyes widen at the same time - to make your point about how big it *really* was. Actors who punctuate a lot with their face often get the criticism that they are too busy or indicating.

Static Face

Your static face is your face when you are not particularly feeling anything at all. Although you are not consciously communicating emotion with your static face, if it has the appearance of emotion on it because of how your face is structured, then those who view you will think you are feeling something when you are not.

I'll be talking more about your static face in the next chapter when we look at the ways we distort the Language of the Face. For now, I wanted to mention it because it is one of the ways your face speaks to others.

The Need to Know the Language of the Face

On-camera directors rely on actors to know the language the face speaks and how to deliver it. Some actors speak it fluently and with ease.

To be in the 5% you must speak this language and recognize it in other performances. It's the language every successful film and TV actor had to learn in order to work consistently. Think of every great scene in a Steven Spielberg film.

Spielberg likes to work with emotions to create and reveal awe, wonderment, excitement, and fear on various levels. These emotions are what make the "Spielberg Face."

In his films, Spielberg uses these emotions – from the most subtle reveal to the more extreme – and skillfully intensifies them with his classic slow or fast push-in of the camera.

Each one of these four emotions – awe, wonderment, excitement, and fear – are similar, yet have distinct subtle differences which makes them not only look different, but feel different.

Although Spielberg uses these four emotions fairly consistently, we don't notice them being repeated because of the actor's unique look and the context in which they appear.

To spot their unique differences, pay close attention to the eyebrows, eyes, and mouth. He also uses a dolly shot to capture the revelation in each of his films with perfection, ending in his trademark close-up, inciting the audience to feel the same sense of awe and wonder that the character experiences.

In *Close Encounters of the Third Kind* there must be at least 30 different shots of awe and wonderment (see photo #24).

#24

Look at Richard Dreyfuss' face in awe (see photo #25) as he is drawn to the spaceship as it attempts to communicate to all that have gathered. You can see his eyes are fixed and his mouth has dropped slightly.

In the *Indiana Jones* movies, Harrison Ford has several moments of shock, which is a mixture of surprise and a negative emotion as well as awe.

#25 #26

In this shot (photo #26), see how his brows are pulled together (low intensity fear), his eyes are widened, and his mouth slightly parted without any tension (surprise). Whatever he is seeing is quite amazing.

Look at Laura Dern's face in *Jurassic Park* (photo #27) as she sees the dinosaurs for the first time. See how her eyes are fixed, her eyelids are raised, and her mouth is just slightly parted.

#27 #28

Dakota Fanning's expression of both fear and surprise (see photo below #28) tells us all about the trauma and unspeakable horrors in *The War of the Worlds*.

Close-ups are meant to manipulate the audience's feelings. But unless what's on the actor's face is recognizable, it will never move them to feel. One thing is for certain, the language of the "Spielberg Face" is recognizable, universal, and moving. If you go to my blog at http:/languageoftheface.blogspot.com/2012/03/want-to-work-in-spielberg-film.html, you can check out Kevin B. Lee's video essay, "The Spielberg Face."

It's not just a director who relies on the actor to communicate thought, feelings, and emotions with their face, but editors as well. One of the biggest frustrations for most editors, from sitcoms to feature films, is not having a reaction from the actor to cut to or from. The actor who has something specific for the editor to work with is the actor who gets screen time.

The Birth of the Emotional Triad

Historically, training for actors has involved learning to use the body and voice to communicate and share what they are feeling and thinking. For stage performances, these two forms of emotional communication have served us well. But since the introduction of on-camera acting, something more intimate was needed – something that can only be seen in medium and close-up shots. I would like to formally introduce you to "The Emotional Triad," which adds a third, very important means of communication for the on-camera actor – your face. This triad of communications between voice, body and face allows you to play in any venue, from the largest stage to the most intimate of settings – the close-up.

When you understand the Language of the Face, are able to speak it correctly and include it with the body and voice, the viewer's understanding of what's happening becomes dramatically clearer. They hear how you feel by the sound of your voice, the tone, rhythm, and intonation. The body tells them how well you're coping with what you feel, by the rhythm of your actions and body posturing. And the face allows them to see exactly what it is that you're feeling.

For the triad to be effective, attention must be paid to all 3 forms of emotional communication: voice, body and face. Your goal as an on-camera actor is to balance this triad. For the master shot, the audience can see what your whole body is doing. They get an indication as to what you are feeling by how you walk, sit, stand, etc. When the shot becomes more intimate, they need to get the information about what you think and feel from your voice and face.

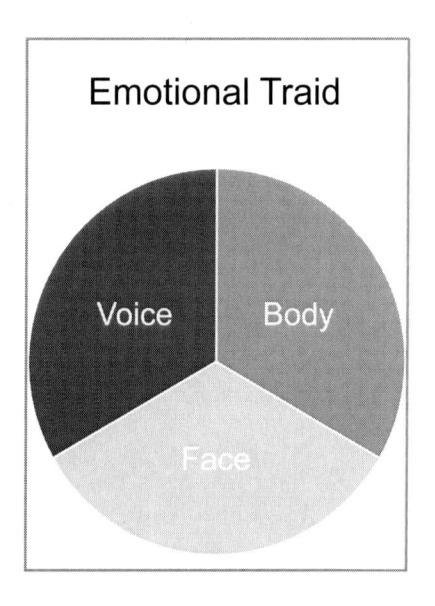

Emotional Traid

Voice | Body | Face

Speaking v. Reading. "The Language of the Face"

It's easy to assume that speaking this emotional facial language is natural and that it happens organically. But the truth is that for an on-camera actor, *reading* this facial language and *speaking* it are two different things. It's like growing up with an Italian speaking grandma. You understand when she asks you in Italian for her shoes or coffee, but you don't speak a word of Italian. How can this be? Over time, you became skilled at recognizing the words she was using and associating them with her requests, but you had no need to learn to speak her language. It's the same with understanding the Language of the Face. You are skilled enough to recognize the emotional language and, in turn, good acting, but you may not be equipped to *speak* it.

In any spoken language, if we give a certain word more emphasis, use the wrong inflection, or use the wrong word entirely, it's very difficult to be understood. The same is true with the Language of the Face – an uplift of the eyebrows, a downward curl of the lip, or the tensing of the muscle around the eyes – all say something very specific. When we do these things without realizing it, it often communicates something different from what we intend.

> *The problem in speaking the Language of the Face is that we were never taught how to do it. We were never given a handbook. Not just as actors, but as human beings. However, the language has always been there...*

What is so misunderstood about the Language of the Face is that when you speak the language clearly, it looks like life – completely natural. And the more skilled an actor becomes at it, the easier it is – and looks. In fact, once you become fluent in the language, it looks like you aren't doing anything at all, which couldn't be further from the truth.

In Patrick Tucker's book, *Secrets of Screen Acting* (2nd edition), he states, "Some experienced actors will make statements along the lines of, 'It has taken me all these years to learn to do nothing on screen – I just think it.' Young actors, reading this, joyfully rush in to do the same and find to their horror that their performances don't exist, they are invisible. This is because the experienced actor now puts her thoughts onto her face without realizing it, and thinks she is doing nothing."

Let's Get Technical

Being completely frank, yes, at first, the process for learning to speak the Language of the Face is technical, similar to learning a sport, dance, or musical instrument. Let's say you've learned to play guitar by ear without really investing in an understanding of music or your instrument. This doesn't mean you can't play. In fact, you might be pretty good. You might even get good enough to get into a band and get some gigs. People may even tell you how good you are.

Then one day you decide that you want to break into the big time, but your style is limited. You find yourself unable to communicate with musicians of a higher caliber. You're unable to talk about music, chords, or beats on the same level. You find yourself envious of what they can do with their instrument.

You realize that if you want to make it, you must totally understand your own instrument and everything you can about music. So, you seek out the best to teach you. Since you've never studied music, the first thing they will teach you are musical scales. "This is a drag," you think. You already know how to play and now you're playing worse because you're thinking about what your fingers are doing. But you are determined to play the big time, so you practice and practice and practice.

You learn all the scales. You learn what specific notes make up what chords, the variations, and types of chords. The chords you knew sound worse because you've had to relearn the proper finger placement. Again, you have to think what your fingers are doing.

You keep practicing and then one day, you notice something. Your fingers are moving up and down the neck of your guitar effortlessly without you even thinking about them. They're hitting all the right notes with ease and clarity. At that moment you realize you no longer have to think about what your fingers are doing because they know what to do. You don't have to worry about playing in the wrong key because your fingers know what key they're playing in without you telling them.

This is the same with emotions and emotional facial expressions. Once you've made the connection, you don't have to think about what your face is doing because it knows what to do. Emotions are like the chords that make up the music we play. The muscle groups are the scales which we must learn and practice.

There's an old joke about a musician asking directions in New York, "How do you get to Carnegie Hall?" The response, "Practice!" And the same is true for you, the on-camera actor. How do you get to the big movie and television studios? You know the answer.

No Face Acting or Mugging, Please!

Absolutely NONE! The emotional expressions that appear on your face must be the direct result of what you feel and think (your opinions). In other words, stimulus/response. When I talk about the Language of the Face, it scares many actors. Some of the first comments I hear from people in my seminars are, "I'll be in my head," "It's too technical," or, "I don't want to worry about what my face is doing."

There are some in this industry who fear that involving the face in acting training would end up in "result" acting or "mugging." To me, being aware of what your face is revealing is no different from being aware of what your body or voice is communicating. Yes, being concerned about what your face is doing can put you in your head the same way being concerned about your body or voice would. The thing is, if you're thinking about what your face or body is doing while you're acting, you're choosing to be in your head at the wrong time. Dealing with physical or emotional facial expressions is something that needs to be taken care of prior to the performance, *not* during.

If you're making a living as an on-camera actor, don't worry about what your face is doing; keep doing what you're doing, because it's working. Having said that, I've had many seasoned actors work with me because they knew the importance of subtle emotional communication.

If you're not making a living as an on-camera actor, your callback ratio is low, or you're not even getting called in, one of the things I would strongly suggest you look at is how your face is communicating. If your emotional communication is real, recognizable, appropriate, and adjustable on demand, your odds of booking are greatly increased.

There are many reasons why your emotional communication may not be working. In the next chapter, I'll be talking about about some of those reasons.

Chapter 5

Why Your Facial Messages May Not Reach Others the Way You Intend

You can't change something unless you have an awareness of what needs correcting.

Here's something I'd like you to think about: if there's a distortion between what you feel and what you reveal on your face, that distortion must be acknowledged, adjusted or compensated for to bring you into alignment and enable you to speak the Language of the Face. Here's what you need to know. It won't change on its own, mostly because what you feel and what you reveal seems absolutely correct and natural to you. It doesn't feel like you're doing anything wrong.

The 7 Ways the Language of the Face Gets Distorted

According to Dr. Ekman, in his book "Unmasking the Face," when an emotion is triggered, emotional facial expressions happen with or without our consent. The most we can do is attempt to manage or distort them. When growing up, we weren't taught about what emotions looked like or felt like, but rather how to manage what we felt. We learned what emotions were appropriate, when we could show them, and how much we could reveal, depending on the situation. Interpretation of this form of communication came through trial and error.

When Mom had a certain look on her face, we learned that it was a good time to ask for more cookies. When Dad looked a certain way, we learned not to bother him until he had time to relax after work. The problem is, if mom had a peculiar way of expressing happiness, or dad had an odd way of expressing irritation and frustration, then more than likely you learned the same expression.

Take a moment to think – is there anyone in your family who is like that? For example, is there someone who has an unusual way of getting angry? When they have a certain expression on their face, does everyone know to stay away? When this person is out in the world, usually no one but family members know what they're feeling if that expression appears on their face.

Has this happened to you? Are people often confused by what and how you express?

There are many reasons your emotional messages may become distorted from what you learn from the people most close to you to your own DNA.

The following seven are the most common and important to the on-camera actor:

- How you're wired
- The culture you were raised in
- Family idiosyncrasies

- Your own psychology
- Inappropriate emotional triggers
- How you listen: literal vs. inferential
- Your face

Let's take a deeper look at each one of these distortions.

How You're Wired

The first way we can distort the Language of the Face is written in our DNA. Personality researchers believe that some people are *internalizers* and others are *externalizers*.

Externalizers are those people who show emotions on their faces but have little change in their autonomic nervous system (ANS). Your ANS controls things like breathing, heart rate, and skin temperature. When an emotion is triggered, changes occur in the nervous system, breathing and heart rate may increase or decrease, and skin temperature may fluctuate. If you're aware of it, the sensations you experience when an emotion is triggered will give you an indication as to where you are in the intensity of that emotion.

Generally, externalizers tend to show more emotion than their body is actually feeling. If you have a problem with consistent facial and/or body movement, conveying a different facial expression for every thought that passes through your mind. Or you are extremely animated about everything (whether you feel intensely about something or not) and are not aware of when this movement is going on, then there's a strong possibility you are an externalizer. Externalizers often hear things like, "You're too busy," "You're showing me what you feel," or "You're indicating."

Internalizers, on the other hand, tend to feel more intensely (higher ANS response) while their faces remain blank.

If this is you, then you're the type of actor who is stone-faced. You give very little to no facial expression. Others are constantly wondering if you hear what they're saying. They want to say to you, "If you like what I'm saying then let your face know, because I haven't got a clue." Internalizers often hear things like, "I know you say you're feeling it, but I'm not getting it," or "It's a lot easier to bring you down than it is to bring you up."

Research has also showed us that as little as 10 hours after birth, some babies are already exhibiting signs of being internalizers or externalizers. This research suggests that some people have learned to hide or reveal their emotions, and some were actually born that way.

How you express yourself on camera, whether it is too big or too small, may not be a psychological problem or a craft problem, but could be a direct result of how you are wired. Your wiring could be at the very core of the challenges you have been facing when it comes to how you express.

Studies indicate that internalizers also tend to be introverts. Externalizers tend to be extroverts. That makes a lot of sense.

I've seen internalizers, in their attempt to come out of their non-expressive shell, become extroverts. The same with externalizers, who in an attempt to stop over-expressing, look like their faces are frozen. Talk about complicating things! Overcompensating is not the answer. Awareness of who you are and how you express is what will help you.

Where the research for these two groups gets really interesting is that they've taken introverts, who are more apt to be internalizers, and extroverts, who are more apt to be externalizers, and hooked them up to a type of lie detector to see just how intensely each was feeling. Under a moderate amount of stimuli, the introvert was actually feeling more intensely than the extrovert, but not expressing it. However, when they raised the stimuli, the introvert emotionally shut down and the extrovert, expressively, calmed down.

What All of This Means to the On-camera Actor?

If you're an internalizer, you tend to feel things pretty intensely already, so when you try to increase the stimulation, you overload and shut down. Have you ever started to prepare for an emotionally charged scene, found the emotion intensifying and all of a sudden you didn't feel anything? Well, you just tripped your emotional circuit breaker and emotionally shut down. If you were to keep adding stimulation, you'd probably find yourself out of control with emotion and on the verge of hysteria.

Actors who know they're internalizers realize that they have to express more, and often try to push it to the limit. If I ask an internalizer to expand the outer expression by adding in more of the emotional facial muscles, they will look at me like I'm crazy. They already feel like they are on the verge of overacting and to go any bigger would push their acting over the edge. They feel absolutely foolish doing what I suggest until they see themselves on camera and witness how what I asked of them made sense. So, matching up the outer expression with the inner intensity is a must if you're an internalizer.

If you're an externalizer, you've probably been told how expressive you are and how everyone knows what you feel and think, and then some! People may have also commented on how your whole demeanor changes when an emotional crisis occurs such as a death, breakup or some other life changing event. In my experience, extreme externalizers are often uncomfortable with real and intense feelings. They tend to shy away from these experiences, especially in their acting. As a way of compensating, they substitute the expression of emotion for the real experience.

In other words, actors who are externalizers know what emotions look like. That makes them great at showing the emotion, especially the bigger ones, although not so good at connecting to the real impulses of the emotion. Considering how they are wired, they need much more stimuli than an internalizer. Without really experiencing the emotion, the externalizer will not have the sensations or the impulses that accompany the emotion they are trying to create.

There is also a third group called generalizers, who show approximately equal increases in expressiveness and ANS response.

> *Research leads me to believe that generalizers make up a big part of the 5% we've been talking about.*

The Culture You Were Raised In

The second means of distorting your desired emotional communication may stem from the culture in which you grew up. Your cultural upbringing can have an impact on all nonverbal communication. Where you were raised plays a big part not only in *how* you display certain emotions, but also *when* and *to what degree*.

Your culture includes the country in which you were raised, as well as your hometown and even your neighborhood. Expression guidelines based on your culture are what Paul Ekman and Wallace Friesen call "Cultural Display Rules."

Every culture has its own display rules. For example, in middle America, most men are taught to manage the appearance of fear and/or sadness; for women, it's anger. Is this something you were taught? If you're a guy, when you experience any fear or sadness in public, how much do you adhere to these rules? If you're a woman, how do you modify or distort your anger? Do you bring these rules into your acting?

Display rules become a real problem for some actors when the material demands or the director requests that you go against them. I often come across male actors who seem to be unable or unwilling to create and communicate fear or sadness. When asked to reveal these emotions, their attempts will most often result in an expression of anger. Other male actors think they're revealing fear, but their faces remain blank. Overcoming conditioning to think, "It's not cool to show anyone that you're afraid," "Being sad is for babies," or, "It's not ladylike to display anger in public" is a real challenge for many.

I've also worked a lot with Asian actors, who often struggle to overcome their cultural display rules. This is especially true of the many native Japanese actors I have worked with over the years. Since respect is such a big part of the Japanese culture, negative emotions are often difficult for many to express. Often out of politeness or respect, they will control the negative emotions they are feeling or replace them with a smile. As you can imagine, this can be a true challenge for these actors.

Adhering to your cultural norms doesn't mean that as an actor you're not capable of experiencing a particular emotion. More than likely you've just been trained to control or modify it and as a result, it wouldn't be a choice you'd make. Why? Expressing it doesn't feel right to you.

Display rules alone aren't a problem for an actor. It's when we adhere to them unknowingly that they can have an impact on what and how much emotion we are willing to reveal.

Think about your own cultural display rules. Is it possible that they are distorting your acting choices?

Family Idiosyncrasies

The third means by which we may distort our emotional communication has its origins in who raised us. "Personal Display Rules," a phrase also coined by Ekman and Friesen, are another set of rules that can challenge how we express emotions. They are the result of our family's idiosyncrasies.

Growing up, you may have heard, "Take that look off your face right now, young lady," or "Don't look at me like that, young man." How about, "Smile at the nice man" – so, as a kid you learned the rules and you smiled at the nice man. Now as an adult, you may still be smiling at the nice man, whether you want to or not. Sometimes you may know you're smiling, but a lot of the time, you don't. Sometimes you can't stop smiling.

Did you grow up with a lot of rules about what you could express and what you could not express? You may be carrying many of those rules with you into your audition. And without your awareness, they could be costing you the job because you are feeling one thing and unconsciously expressing another. Or, perhaps, you're feeling the sensations of an emotion but failing to reveal it.

Again, I suggest you think about how your family's idiosyncrasies may be distorting what you intend to reveal and impacting your acting.

Your Own Psychology

The fourth way that your emotional communications can be distorted is based on your own psychology. I'm not implying that any one person's psychology is distorted. Rather, I want to point out how your experiences and observations over time can be responsible for how you perceive and react to a given event. Your own unique experiences and observations have helped form your beliefs. When something of importance happens in your life, these beliefs clue you in on how you should behave, what you should think, and even how you should feel. These beliefs are often responsible for what an actor is willing or not willing to emotionally reveal.

> *Your experiences have the power to enhance or distort how you see the world and everything in it.*

For an on-camera actor, your experiences may not only distort how you express emotion, but also how you interpret material. Your emotional attachments to events that have happened in the past have a way of altering the reality of what's happening in the present. For example, say you grew up with an overpowering father who would often burst out in rage, scaring the hell out of you. This past event may alter how you express yourself when confronted by an angry person. You may find that every time you're in a scene where you're face to face with someone angry, you shut down or start to cry, even though the scene is calling for you to respond with anger. Even though you try to create the anger, your connection to the past event is much too strong and triggers an unwanted emotion. This distortion of what you are trying to express may sometimes work for you, say, if the character was vulnerable or scared, but not if you were playing a hard-nosed district attorney.

What you are sensitive to and how you perceive the world and the events in it are dictated by your own psychology. If you're unaware of how your personal psychology is influencing you to react in an inappropriate way, the viewer will be confused.

If an event like this is in your past, you obviously can't completely erase it, as much as you might like to. But your awareness of it and how it may be affecting your acting is critical so you can make the necessary adjustments.

Inappropriate Triggers

The fifth way you may distort what you are trying to emotionally communicate is by unknowingly choosing stimuli that are inappropriate for what is taking place. Consciously, you believe you feel one way, but unconsciously you feel something else. You might believe you were angry about a breakup, but the truth is you really feel sad. So, while you're focusing on what you think will make you angry, your face is revealing the truth about how you really feel.

Real v. Appropriate

Knowing the difference between being real and being appropriate may save you from having a very bad day at an audition. It's one of the biggest lessons an on-camera actor has to learn.

As we've already established, being real is acting and reacting with enough detail to make it look like life. We've also established that being appropriate means your actions and reactions are suitable or proper for the circumstances requested of you. Many believe that if you're real, you'll automatically be appropriate. The fact is – you can be real *and* inappropriate at the same time.

Let me give you an example. I asked one of my students to take a sip of her coffee and find it slightly bitter. She took a sip and the reaction she gave was as if it was the most disgusting thing she had ever tasted. I asked her if she heard the direction I gave. I repeated, "I need a real response to slightly bitter," and she replied, now with even more disgust on her face, "I *was* being real, I hate bitter."

The actor's inappropriate response wasn't based on how she was wired to express or any particular display rules to which she was adhering. She heard my direction correctly, so she didn't misinterpret it based on how she listens. The distortion was the result of using an *inappropriate trigger* for the distaste request.

Her response was based on her opinion or experience of something bitter. Her opinion of a bitter taste was so strong there was very little she could do to adjust it. Just hearing the word "bitter" caused a fairly big reaction of disgust in her. In order for this actress to stay real to herself, as well as appropriate to the viewer, she is going to have to either modify the amount of her imagined bitter taste or choose a more appropriate stimulus.

As an actor who is creating real, recognizable, appropriate emotional facial expressions, especially in the audition setting, it is imperative you know what emotion you are going to experience and express. To what degree and how you will trigger that emotion is key. If you consciously or unconsciously use the wrong emotional trigger, you may not get the result you desired or more importantly, the one that is being asked of you.

Here's the thing. If you have an extreme sensitivity to stimuli that most people don't, you won't appear real. Conversely, if your opinion or experience of something is extremely less than what would normally occur, you also risk being inappropriate. Today, especially in commercial auditions, no matter how true you feel a response is, if it's interpreted by the viewer as inappropriate, you will most likely be seen as not being real.

How You Listen

The sixth way you may distort what you are trying to communicate emotionally is how you take in information. There is a great deal of research to support the fact that people take in information in two ways – literally and inferentially.

Literal listeners take the things they hear at face value and don't read anything into what is said. They take the words very literally.

Inferential listeners, on the other hand, will try to work out what they think was meant by what was said, put their own interpretation on it, and often assume it implies some action that needs to be taken by them. For example, someone may say to a literal listener, "The room is cold," and the literal listener may respond with, "Yes, it is." Whereas the inferential listener may respond with, "Would you like me to turn the heat up?" Why is this information important for an actor to know? Because how we listen is critical to how we take in and filter information.

If you're an actor who hears literally, often you don't pick up the nonverbal or subtle messages given by casting or a director. You struggle with analogies and metaphors. You are most confident when someone tells you exactly what to do.

What I call "romantic language," which I talked about earlier is constructed to inspire or provoke an emotional response from an actor will often shut down an actor who is a literal listener. Why? Because romantic language is inferential. For example, a director may say to you, "It's like when your girlfriend broke up with you," or "Do it like you have to take a pee." Yes, that last example is a true story. One of my students got that very direction in an audition! Romantic language is filled with metaphors and analogies. Unless the literal listening actor can connect the direction to what is actually happening, they will often find themselves confused.

With respect for the actor's process, many casting directors and directors don't want to tell you *what* to feel or *how* to reveal it. But even if they do, the literal actor may get lost if the direction isn't specific enough. The literal actor seeks clarity before they can act. So many times during the casting process (either by myself or with a director), I've experienced giving direction to an actor only to see them at a total loss as to what to do with the information. It's not because they're bad actors or I wasn't being clear, it's just that they couldn't comprehend and process what was being asked of them.

If you're an actor who hears inferentially, you're not quite off the hook. When given a literal direction you might miss it all together. An inferential actor quickly deduces directions and comes up with a game plan. Ready to go! The problem is that often they miss some of the facts. Inferential actors often try to interpret all the suggestions. Did she mean this? Did he mean that? Quickly you can go into overload with an infinite amount of possibilities.

In my years of casting, I often witnessed an inferential listening actor receive a specific direction – not once, but sometimes three times. And each time they got the direction, they did something other than what was asked of them. Talk about us all speaking a different language!

How we take in and filter information is critical to creating real, recognizable, appropriate, emotional facial expressions.

Inferential and literal listening brings us back to how we use our emotional triggers. If we misinterpret the information, we are more apt to use the wrong trigger. If we use the wrong trigger, we'll likely get the wrong response. To complicate things even more, most people also lean towards *speaking* in a literal or inferential manner. What that means is sometimes the speaker (casting or a director, for example) wants you to do exactly what they're saying and sometimes they want to hint about it. On top of all that, stress during an audition can often intensify your style of listening.

Your Face

Based on how your face is structured, people who view you might think you're feeling something that you're not. That is the seventh distortion.

"I'm not mad, sad, upset, or worried. I'm listening." Have you ever had to say that to someone?

Out of all the ways we can possibly distort the expression of what we feel, your face may have the greatest impact of them all. Have you ever thought about what your face is saying to others when you're just thinking or listening? Most haven't.

If you've ever had to speak in front of a group of people and you look out at those in the crowd, you've likely witnessed a sea of faces that look bored, who you think dislike you or are feeling sorry for you, or are unexplainably very enthusiastic. It's a very strange feeling.

Hundreds of actors have come to my studio unaware that how they were seeing themselves was not the same way casting was seeing them, either by looking at their headshot or in person. How often have you thought someone was a snob or stuck up, then when you get to know them saw that what you originally thought was the furthest from the truth? How could we be so misunderstood?

Facial structure, emotional protection, long term history of an emotion or the lingering of a present emotion can alter or contribute to the appearance of your face. These alterations are chiefly responsible for the misinterpretation or distortion of your facial communication.

Static Face

As I mentioned in the last chapter, your static face can be responsible for the appearance of emotion even when you're not particularly feeling anything at all.

"I'm not bad; I'm just drawn that way." – Jessica Rabbit

For some people, the structure of their face resembles an emotion. For example, a low brow with deep-set eyes may look like anger. Or the pulling down of the corners of the lips might make a person appear sad. There are other ways emotion can become etched on your face.

Default Face/ Emotionally Protecting Yourself

Over time, you may have learned to cover an emotion you were feeling with another emotion you weren't feeling. For example, if you didn't want everyone to know you were frightened, you might cover it by displaying an angry face. Or maybe in an attempt to hide your insecurities, you try to get others to think you're superior, so you learned to wear a look of contempt.

Even in what you might think as a neutral state, your face may look like you're feeling something, and hence thinking something, even when you're not. It's important to know if this is true for you. Do people frequently ask you, "Are you okay?" or "Is anything wrong?" Do people tend to feel intimidated or condescended to by you? If so, you're one of those people I'm talking about.

I would like to draw a distinction between someone's static look and default look. Your static look is the result of bone structure – how your eyes are set in your head or how the face has been re-formed after a long period of experiencing an emotion. Your default look, on the other hand, is the look you have when you want to feel comfortable or safe. It's your "go to" expression. More than likely, it's the look you bring into your audition with you.

Emotional History

Emotions are expressed with muscle groups. If you've been experiencing an emotion for a long time, you've been using the muscle groups associated with that emotion. After a while, those muscles become etched on your face. Your mother might have told you, "Don't keep making that face, or it could stay that way." She may have been right.

Lingering Emotion

If you just experienced an emotional event, even though that event is now over, the emotion you experienced may still be hanging around on your face without your awareness. For example, you may have had a fight with your boyfriend or girlfriend right before your audition. When you go in to meet the casting director, you may not be aware that some of the anger is still showing on your face. Not a good first impression!

What does this mean to the on-camera actor?

Having the appearance of emotion on your face has an impact on how people read you and who they expect you to be. There are other ways this may impact your acting success:

- It can color or even distort other emotions you are trying to reveal.

- Without knowing it, you may be intensifying an emotion that is already on your face, making the response bigger than you think.

- Casting expects you to be what you project on your headshot and in person. For example, your face shows signs of anger, so you look like you would have a determined or aggressive personality. But as soon you open your mouth, you reveal a shy or timid nature. Your headshot is not revealing who you really are.

Take a look at the individual actors in the photo below (#29). Do you see a hint of distaste, fear, contempt, disgust, awe, or pleasure on any of their faces? Who would you say is feeling or thinking and who is neutral?

#29

Answer: None of these actors claimed to be feeling anything particular at the time. They were just being neutral in a listening state.

Some faces talk a little bit, some talk a lot. Some faces just don't shut up. Knowing what your face is already communicating to others, without consciously adding a thing, is critical to your on-camera success. What is your face saying?

If you look at Jordan, the actor on the far left, you may notice that he looks challenging and aggressive. This is because of his jutting jaw and arched brows. The jutting jaw is in the anger family. The arched brow is more of an emblem of questioning.

Sabrina, the actor next to Jordan, looks fearful. This is because of the slight tension in her lower eyelids and the slight widening of her eyes. Both muscle groups are in the fear family.

JT, to the right of Sabrina, looks a bit bewildered because of the slight parting of his lips, his jaw dropping, and his upper eyelids being raised. Those muscle groups are in the surprise family.

Tamara, on the far right, looks disinterested, bored, or judgmental. This is the result of her raised brows, an emblem for questioning or doubt, and the appearance of the clamped corner of her mouth, which looks like contempt.

What Does this All Mean to the On-camera Actor?

Looking back at all the distortions, you can see how they may not only have a hand in making what you reveal inappropriate, but also why you may not appear to be real to the viewer.

The "real you" may be determined by any one or combination of the distortions we just covered, for example:

- Your wiring: I'm an excessively expressive actor who tends to show every thought and feeling, or I'm an actor who feels intensely but keeps it to myself.
- Your culture: I'm an actor who responds in accordance to what my culture deems appropriate.
- Family idiosyncrasies: I'm an actor who smiles no matter what I really feel.
- Your own psychology: I'm an actor who doesn't reveal anything that may embarrass me, including revealing my real feelings or opinions.
- How you listen: I'm an actor who has the potential to misinterpret everything you say, or I'm an actor who needs to be told exactly how to behave.

Personal Inventory – Your Distortion Checklist

☐   Check off all the statements that apply to you.

- ☐ Static face: people often think I'm feeling something when I'm not.
- ☐ My face is very expressive and shows everything I feel.
- ☐ My face shows very little of what I actually feel.
- ☐ Cultural upbringing: my cultural background has a strong influence on me.
- ☐ Family rules: my family instilled very strong beliefs in me about what emotions I can or should show in public.
- ☐ Personal beliefs: my beliefs are often in conflict or out of proportion with others.
- ☐ Choosing inappropriate triggers: I often have trouble figuring out what I feel.
- ☐ I hear literally.
- ☐ I hear inferentially.

Any one of these ways of managing or distorting can have a negative impact on either what you are trying to emotionally create or facially reveal. The more boxes you check, the greater potential you have for distorting how you communicate emotions, feelings, and thoughts. Speaking the Language of the Face requires you to not only have an understanding of what you respond to emotionally and why, but how you personally reveal emotion.

Now that you have a better understanding of the science of emotions and how you might distort what you're trying to create and/or express, let's tackle four of the contemporary beliefs about how the 5% achieved the results they did. Let's see if they are truths, misconceptions, or have just been misguided attempts to define the Language of the Face.

Chapter 6

Myths and Misconceptions about On-Camera Acting

In chapter 3, we discussed that the biggest difference between stage and on-camera acting is in how we communicate emotion. Stage uses the body and voice; on-camera acting uses the body, voice and *face*. In chapter 2, we defined the combination of those 3 methods of communication as the "Emotional Triad." We've also established that the 5% have the skill to interpret sides, copy, or direction and turn it into real, recognizable, appropriate, and repeatable emotional facial reactions, often on demand.

Let's address and demystify some of the challenges and frustrations in making the transition from stage to screen. With that goal in mind, we'll determine if the current beliefs about on-camera acting solve the problem or potentially create new ones.

The current beliefs:

- On-camera acting is about making everything smaller.
- It's all in the eyes.
- Think the thought and the camera will pick it up.
- Just be honest.

Making Everything Smaller

Many acting teachers, as well as actors, believe that the 5% achieves the results they do by making everything smaller. In fact, there are many acting classes whose mission is to make every actor suited for on-camera work by reducing the actor's physical, vocal, and emotional expression. To be clear, making everything smaller translates into, "use the same tools and do the same acting you do on stage, and just make it smaller." There are also some casting directors and directors who consider smaller to be more "real." But is smaller actually more real? Or is it more appropriate to what is happening at the moment? Or is it just more appropriate to the style of the show they're casting, or the spot they're directing?

30

For example, if they were casting or directing one of the CSI crime dramas (photo #30 right side) or a more intimate TV commercial where they might use a lot of ECU's (Extreme Close-Ups), intimate acting is a must. However, would they want the same style of acting if they were casting a teen comedy movie, sitcom or any of the TV shows you might see on Disney Plus (photo #30 left side)? Probably not.

Although they want and need your acting to be real, the style is anything but small. The actor whose emotional facial expression is real yet fails to adjust to make it appropriate for the style of the shows I just mentioned, will have trouble working in those markets.

So, the question we need to answer is, does making everything smaller help you to create and reveal real, recognizable, appropriate, emotional facial reactions?

If you're part of the 5%, making it smaller is a valid adjustment because you're already revealing real and recognizable facial reactions. The next step for them is to make their reactions more appropriate by making them smaller. But if you're not in the 5%, the answer is – no, making everything smaller is not the answer, because you don't necessarily have the appropriate facial reactions from the start. It's like singing off key. No matter how loud or soft you sing, if you're flat, you're flat. Volume doesn't matter.

If you're not in the 5%, the "make everything smaller" adjustment may be more frustrating than helpful to achieve the desired result. The reason? Stage acting not only uses the body and voice to communicate emotion, but also relies on both to create and sustain the emotion. Most actors trained for the stage have learned that if they do something with the correct intention and intensity, it will lead them to feel something. For example, if you behave in an angry manner, take the actions of an angry person and inflect your voice with an angry tone (such as yelling or growling) you will feel, look and sound like an angry person. This works wonderfully for the stage.

Why? It reads big enough and real enough for everyone to see and hear.

Think about this. If you use your body and voice to create, intensify, or sustain emotion, logically it would make sense that when you make the voice and body smaller you also reduce the emotional intensity. This is why most actors are emotionally alive when they speak or take action, but lose all connection to the emotion when they are still. The face is blank. So, just making your stage acting smaller for an on-camera reaction shot, for example, will not result in the outcome you desire.

A young actress confided in me that her conservatory acting teachers were at a loss at what to do with her. When she came to them, although they enjoyed her work, they felt her acting was too big for on-camera work and kept adjusting her to be smaller. By the time she got to the end of the course they told her that her acting had become boring and she should forget everything they had told her. Talk about frustrating!

In her case, what she was doing when she started her training was appropriate for the stage. It worked. She had tons of stage experience to back it up. However, when she tried to make what she was doing smaller for on-camera to please her teachers, she soon discovered that she was failing to communicate anything. She was stifling every impulse she had to express; she only knew how to express those impulses through her body and voice. She didn't have the tools to turn those impulses into real, recognizable, appropriate emotional facial reactions. As a result, she became boring as an on-camera actor.

Does the dilemma of this young actress sound familiar to you? Are you one of the many who have walked out of an audition after a casting director kept insisting you make what you were doing smaller until it finally all disappeared and then concluded, "I guess film acting is about doing nothing?"

On-camera acting is *not* about "doing nothing." Nothing looks like, well... nothing. Here's the catch: some people can get away with doing what seems like nothing because signs of emotion are already etched on their face. As we've already established, a person's static face, without doing anything, may look like they're sad, upset, worried, excited, or a host of other emotions (refer back to photo #29). I'm sure you've met people like this, or perhaps this is you and you've been unaware of what your face is actually saying to others. Unless you have an expressive static look, when you do nothing, trust me, it looks like nothing.

If on-camera acting was a matter of taking what you do on stage and making it smaller, logic would suggest that an on-camera actor who has never been on the stage could just make things bigger and have success in the theatre. This just wouldn't work. Odds are no one would be able to hear her, because she hasn't been trained to project her voice to a large house.

We likely wouldn't have a clue as to what she wanted or what she was feeling either. She would need to understand how to emotionally express herself physically, with body language as well as the voice. Because on-camera acting often requires more stillness in the body, her expressions and actions would be much too small for the stage.

No matter how big you make still, still is still – still...

To make my point even clearer, if you told an acoustic band playing for a small house, "If you want to be heard playing at Dodger Stadium, just strum harder and sing louder," that would not only be bad advice, it would be insane. Strumming harder and singing louder just won't work. It's a different venue. They need different tools to be heard. They need amplifiers, microphones, etc. It's the same with on-camera acting.

As an on-camera actor, you need to acquire the tools that will give you control of what you're communicating. These tools make it possible for you to adjust the expression of what you feel to be appropriate for the style of any particular show or venue.

My suggestion is not to be so concerned with bigger or smaller – that's stage thinking. Your concern should be about what's *appropriate* for the moment – that's on-camera thinking.

It's All in the Eyes

We've all heard the saying, "the eyes are the windows to the soul." Acting, they say, is all in the eyes. In fact, I've seen photographers pleading with actors to bring it to their eyes, acting teachers working in vain to get an actor to create an emotion and push it through their eyes, and casting directors claiming that all good acting is in the eyes.

One of the reasons the 5% are considered to be so successful is the belief that they're able to move emotion through their eyes.

> *The reality is – you can't push an emotion through your eyes!*

Scientifically speaking, there is no conduit from your eyes to the emotional peptides in your body. It doesn't exist. Let's think logically for a moment. Have your eyes ever gotten angry? Have your eyes ever woken you up in the middle of the night saying, "Damn, I'm mad?" Obviously, the answer is no.

Here's what your eyes can do. Your pupils can dilate or contract, which can be a sign of excitement. Your eyes can move left to right, up and down, and around in circles. They can do this fast or slow. They can focus in on something or someone. They may get wet or dry, but that could also be allergies.

So, the question is, if it's not all in the eyes, where is it?

4 Main Ways the Eyes Speak to the Camera

Although we may focus on someone's eyes, we're taking in more information than we realize. We also pick up the slight, relaxed opening of someone's mouth (which is in the family of surprise- see photo #10) or their eyebrows being pulled slightly down and drawn together (which is in the family of anger- see photo #14).

As you learned in chapter 3, there are certain muscles and muscle groups on the face that are connected to specific emotions. However, that's just the tip of the iceberg. It doesn't take much to change the whole look of your face. Just the slightest contraction, expansion, or tension of any one muscle belonging to any one of the 7 universal emotions changes the whole appearance of the face, making it look like it's all in the eyes (see photos #9 and #10).

Your eyes may be the windows to your soul, but it's your eyebrows and eyelids that are the workhorses of nonverbal communication. In the photos below are four common messages your eyelids send the viewer and what they convey on film. Look carefully at the brow and or eyelid and see if you pick up the message being sent.

#31

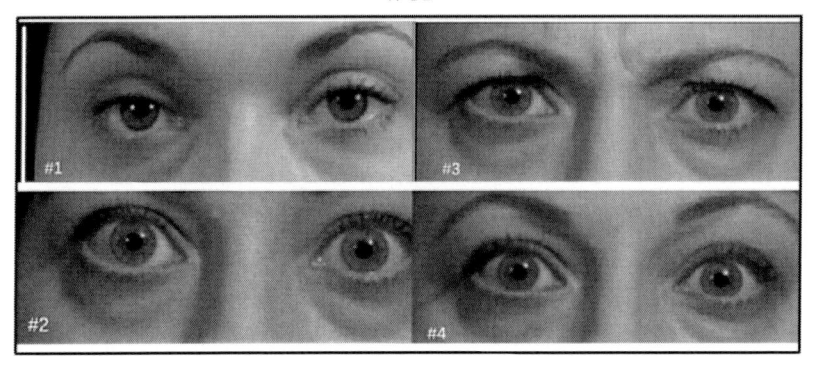

- Photo #31, top left #1: Depending on the circumstances and a person's facial structure, if the upper eyelids relax and droop, it can read as a sign of being slightly sad, tired or bored. These changes happen around the eyes and to the eyelids, but they have very little to do with the eyeballs themselves.

- Photo #31, top left #2: Depending on the circumstances, when the eyes just widen without any tension, it's a sign of some kind of interest – positive or negative.

- Photo #31, top right #3: On the other hand, if the lids get tense, it might be the beginning of anger or intense focus on something, especially if the eyebrows are drawn together and down.

- Photo #31, bottom right #4: When the bottom eyelids are tense and the upper eyelids are raised, exposing the white above the pupils, it's a sign that you may be experiencing the beginning of fear.

Don't Confuse the Viewer

If there is overall tension in the face and the eyes are fixed, it may appear to the viewer that the actor is experiencing something, though more than likely the viewer will be unclear as to what that something is.

To intensify this, if an actor's static face already has the appearance of emotion, we begin to read more into it. Say their static face has a hint of sadness or disgust, and the eyes are fixed and focused. Then you may interpret the fixed and focused eyes with the appearance of emotion, determining that they are feeling something when in actuality that may not be the case.

> *The 5% either have an awareness of what their static faces are saying and know how to use it – or they're able to intuitively make subtle adjustments.*

Other Ways Your Eyes Speak To the Camera

Eye movement can tell the viewer a lot about your current emotional or cognitive state. It can also inform the viewer about status and intentions.

Although there are several types of movements to explore, the following 3 ways will be the most helpful when you are working in front of the camera.

Eyes looking up

Looking up towards the left or or right can be signs of cognitive activity. You're recalling or imagining something. It might be a party you attended or imagining what it would be like to go to a party (see photo #32).

#32

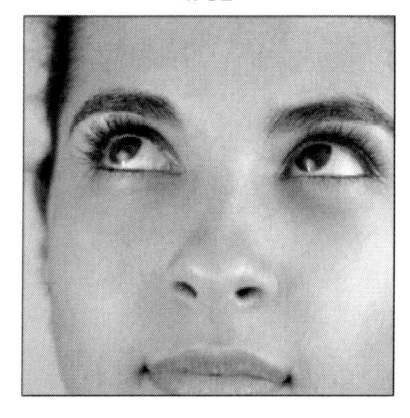

Looking up *without* the cognitive activity can send a signal of boredom, judgment or both (photo #33).

#33   #34

Eyes Looking to the side

We often look towards one ear when we are recalling sound and the other when imagining a sound. For example, you recall the sound of someone's voice or imagining that voice under different circumstances (see photo #34).

Eyes Looking down

Positioning yourself so you are looking down upon someone sends a message of dominance or trying to establish dominance.

#35 #36

Tilting your head back so that you look down your nose sends a signal of judgment or superiority (see photo #35).

Looking down can be read as a sign of submission or guilt.

Depending on the context, it may be a humble/helpless submission, reluctant or even one of angry submission (see photo #36).

Gazing

Gazing is an important body language tool. When you gaze, you look at something continuously consciously or unconsciously, often with little to no blinking. It has our attention. It can be a hard gaze of anger directed towards someone or something or a soft gaze reserved for more intimate moments.

Here's the thing about gazing. Looking at something shows an interest in it, whether it's a person or thing, near or far. Something or someone has your attention.

When you gaze at something, others who look at your eyes will feel compelled to follow your gaze to see what you are looking at. This a great tool. Conversely, if nothing has your attention, your connection with the viewer diminishes. Employing the gaze also gives you more options than just forcing eye contact. There are three types of gazing that involve a person: Social, Intimate and Power.

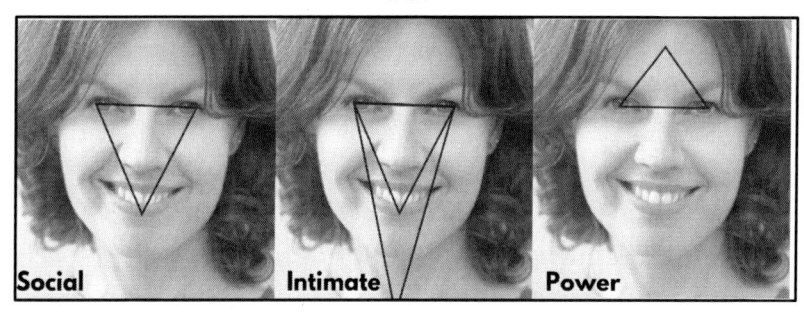

#37

- **Social Gazing** – This gaze forms a triangle between the eyes and the mouth. It is non-aggressive and shows comfort or interest in the person or conversation. Most often you'll take advantage of this zone when listening (see photo #37 far left).

- **Intimate Gazing** – This gaze is similar to the social gazing, which involves the eyes and mouth, however, it tends to be more soft or diffused, and gently moves back and forth from eyes to mouth. Something to note- The moment can quickly move from love to lust if the gaze moves lower to the body (see photo #37 center).

- **Power Gazing** – This is a triangle between the eyes and the forehead. It avoids the intimate areas of the mouth and body completely. This gaze can be quite insulting and hence indicate a position of presumed dominance, as the person effectively says, "I am more powerful than you, your feelings are unimportant to me and you will submit to my gaze." (See photo #37 far right.) Looking at their forehead or not at them at all indicates disinterest. This may also be shown by defocused eyes where the person is "inside their head," thinking about other things.

Gazing Exercise

After going through all the different messages your eyes can send, I suggest you try them out. Find a partner. Set up some circumstances where each type of gaze you're working on would make sense.

Keep it simple, ask your partner talk about their day. As they do, work each gaze. Do each one individually. Start with the social, after a few moments, stop and set up the intimate. Then stop, set up the power gaze.

Once you are engaged, pay close attention to how each gaze makes you feel. To determine if you are doing them correctly, as you move from one gaze to the other, there should be slight changes to how you feel and think about your partner.

Masking Your Face

As I've already shared, we take in more information than what the eyes reveal. That truth has never been more evident than now. At the time of writing this 2nd edition, we are in the middle of a global pandemic and encouraged to wear masks in order to slow down the spread of the virus.

The wearing of masks has created all sorts of communication problems. And these problems all stem from the fact that we can't get enough information from the face, because much of the face is covered, except for the eyes.

Just seeing the eyes is not enough to pick up the subtleties of how a person feels or what they are thinking. Another way of looking at it would be, wearing a mask sends us back to stage acting. In order to communicate, we are all forced to add more body language and vocal cues.

Take a look at photo#38 below. I took all the subtle photos that we have already seen and put masks on them. See if you can still determine the subtle emotion under the mask. You can look down at photo #39 to see if you're correct.

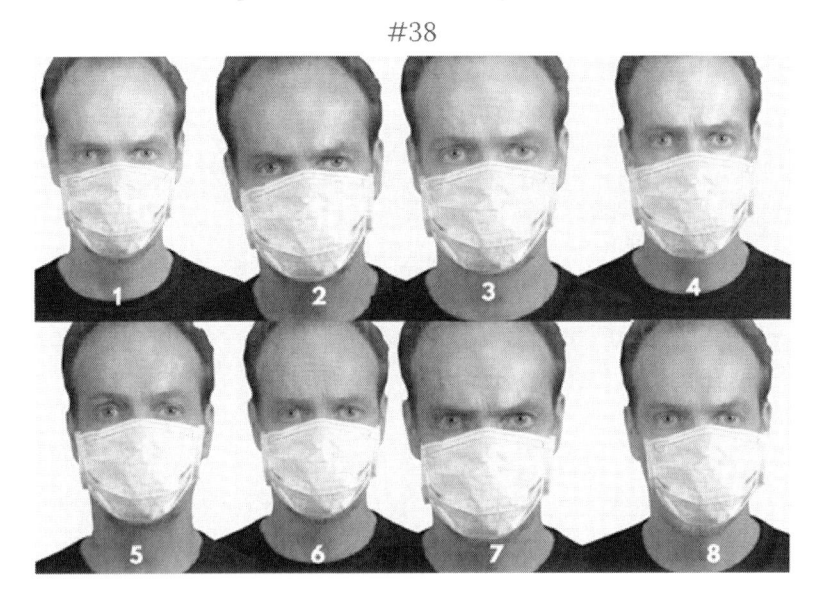

#38

#39

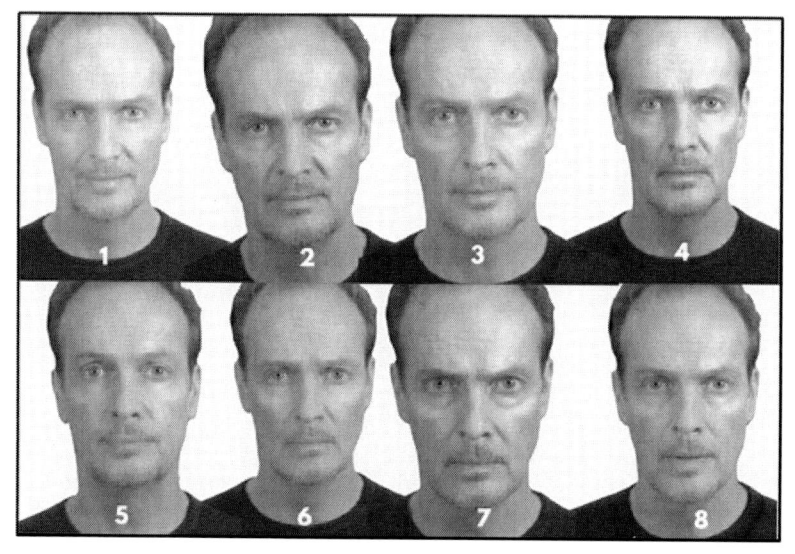

Photo #39 answers: 1:Joy / 2:Disgust / 3:Neutral / 4:Fear / 5:Contempt / 6:Sad / 7:Anger / 8:Surprise

Say Hello To Your Eyebrows

Earlier I said, your eyebrows and eyelids are the workhorses of nonverbal communication, However, not everyone understands or agrees with me.

So often I hear people in the industry tell actors that if they want to work on-camera, they'd better learn to keep their eyebrows from moving, as well as the rest of their face.

An actress who was taping a scene for her demo reel once told me she was scolded by her director for moving her eyebrows. He told her she needed to learn to not move anything on her face and say the lines as quickly as possible.

I'm not going to comment at this point on saying the lines quickly. However, making a blanket statement like, "Don't move anything on your face," was not helpful. In fact, this direction scarred her until she came to me and began to understand that her brows are an intricate part of communication.

The truth is that the brows should move when it's *appropriate* for the brows to move, just like every other on-camera action needs to be deliberate.

If not moving the eyebrows is what film acting is about, apparently no one told some Academy Award winning actors about it. Take a look at each of the following photos and try to imagine what these wonderful actors would look like if only their eyes were involved. Would they be as powerful?

As you study each photo, bring focus to what the eyebrows, eyelids, cheekbones, and lips are doing and see how it helps the viewer to understand and interpret what the actor is feeling and thinking.

Look at Tom Hanks (photo #40) in this hugely memorable moment in *Castaway*. Without his eyebrows positioned the way they are, combined with the raising of his cheeks in pain, would you still feel the loss and worry he was experiencing when he lost Wilson?

40

What about Natalie Portman's (photo #41) captivating performance in *Black Swan*? Would you still feel her fear and surprise if her eyebrows didn't raise and slightly pull together, while her eyes widened with slight tension in the bottom eyelids and her mouth dropped open and slightly pulled back? I don't think so!

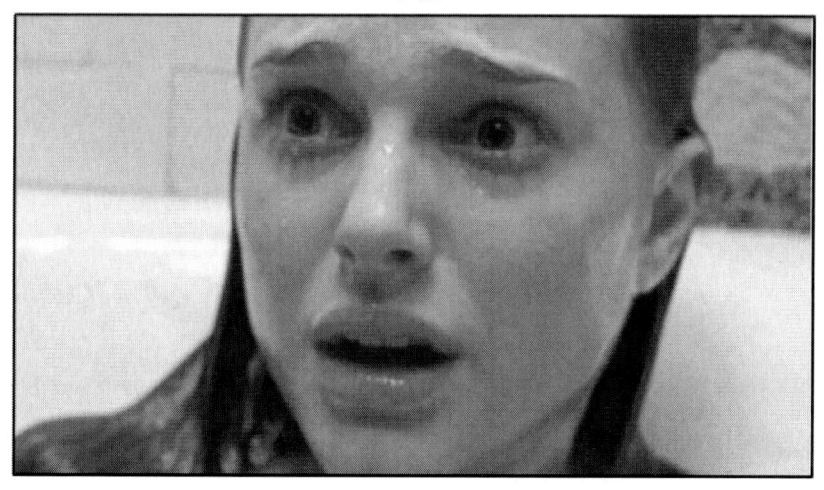

#41

Look at photo #42. In Adrian Brody's moving performance in *The Pianist*, even without knowing the story, you immediately feel what is on his face – loss, longing, and sadness. Although you mainly see this from the inner corners of his eyebrows lifting up, there are also signs in the heaviness of the eyelids and the slight pushing up of his lower lip.

42

Denzel Washington (photo #43) is an *incredibly* powerful actor. His face is anything but static. In this photo you can see all the messages going on – it's the face of a man who has been hurt. His brows are raised in some kind of question or doubt.

43

You can see the hint of sadness in the lower part of his mouth. This is coming from the bottom lip raising up, causing that dimple on his chin. Yet there's a sign of strength that comes from his jaw slightly jutting out.

If you've been working on the assumption that you can push your thoughts through your eyes or telepathically communicate what you're feeling by staring at another person, it might be time to rethink that belief. Often, in auditions, I see actors attempting to do exactly that. But if your face remains blank while you feel an eruption going on inside, no one will ever know it. Your thoughts must reach your face in order for them to be read by the viewer.

The myth that "it's all in the eyes" also has an impact on the photos you take. Since your face is not changing, you will be limited to either capturing your default look, which is the face you use to protect yourself, or a look that is forced and disingenuous. Either way, unless you know how the face speaks and how to speak with it, you will continue to take the same shots over and over again.

Think the Thought and the Camera Will Pick It Up

Any qualified acting teacher will tell you that you have to have thought. That is what motivates us to physical and verbal action, as well as colors the tone of our words. But can thought alone be the tool that guides you to real, recognizable, and appropriate emotional facial reactions? Apparently for the 5% it does. We see that when we view them without sound. Then, why is it so hard for the 20% to achieve the same result? Perhaps there's more to the story.

Having a Strong Connection

In order for your thought to manifest on your face appropriately, you must have a strong enough idea, opinion or emotional connection to what you're thinking. And you must be in alignment with what you feel and what your face reveals. Otherwise, the thought will never register on your face.

You have many thoughts every day. Most are not strong enough to change the appearance of your face. For example, take a moment and think about what you did so far today. If the morning is fresh in your mind and nothing eventful happened, thinking about it won't cause a change, subtle or otherwise, to your face. It will remain in its static state. If you're having trouble concentrating or the events of the morning were unclear, your brows may have just pulled together slightly or there may have been some slight tension in your eyelids or the ridge of your lips.

These cognitive facial reactions would be the result of trying to remember the morning, but not your opinions or feelings about the morning. If something eventful did happen, that would be different.

Let's say that this morning, half asleep, you walked out from your bedroom in your cowboy pajamas that are just a tad too small, making you look a little silly. With your hair a mess, you walk into the kitchen and come face to face with the plumber your roommate let in to fix the sink.

Recalling this event, depending on how strongly you felt at the time or how strong of an opinion you have about the event, an emotional reaction would more than likely register on your face, maybe something like embarrassment or regret.

On the other hand, if this event didn't bother you, why would you react when recalling it? If your face reacts without real opinion or emotional connection to the event, then what you are doing is showing the viewer that you're just thinking, as opposed to having real, emotional or opinionated thoughts.

> *Thought, not connected to a strong enough idea, opinion or emotion, will often leave the face blank and devoid of any emotional expression.*

The way to ensure successful and recognizable transmission of thought is to understand the emotional connection you have to opinions, ideas, and events that are taking place and to understand what they feel like and look like on your face. This emotional connection is what the camera *does* pick up. For example, a hint of anger may be revealed by the slight tension in your eyelids or ridge of the lips. Dislike or displeasure may be revealed by the raising of the upper lip or the slight wrinkling of the nose. To understand the emotional connection, here again, you must understand emotions themselves – what triggers them and what they look like and feel like on your face.

> *An emotional expression not connected to a thought is an acting lie.*

While working with actors on their auditions, not only beginners but seasoned actors as well, I find what's missing in their work is history connected to the situation that is taking place or the words they are speaking. When there is no history, the words lack color and the face often remains blank.

How do we read a character's history?

Although we're speaking primarily about the face, we can read a character's history through any one of the emotional triad components. When someone has a strong emotional connection with their thought, subtle changes take place in the voice, body and/or facial expression. For example, if there is sadness intertwined with their thought, their voice may get lower and/or softer. Their body may reflect heaviness or a dropping of the head. On their face, the inner corner of their eyebrows may raise, or the corners of their lips may pull down.

When any one of these changes occurs, in combination with the words that are spoken, these triad messages inform the viewer how you feel about what you're saying. When the words contradict what your emotional messages are displaying, then the viewer reads the subtext or the true meaning behind the words. Changes in the body, voice and more specifically, the face, can inform the viewer of a character's likes, dislikes, sensitivities, desires, etc.

Where does this history come from?

Specific ideas, opinions and/or judgments rooted in the character's past are in some way connected to what's happening in the present. As an actor, your job is to discover a character's history and to know what those opinions or feelings are. You can find information in the script by noticing what other characters say about your character, the things your character does or doesn't do, etc. When little information is provided, you still need to make choices about your character's relevant past in order to create and reveal history.

We reveal our history constantly in our daily life, often in the most subtle ways. My favorite example is when your friend asks if you want to grab a bite to eat. When he mentions the name of the restaurant, your upper lip rises toward your nose slightly or your nose wrinkles just a bit as you shake your head, "nah." At that moment, you reveal your history with that restaurant based on your past experience. In this case, it's a negative one. Perhaps you didn't like the food or the servers.

Either way, your face reacted with a look of slight disgust or distaste.

Not only would your friend instantly know that you didn't want to go to that particular restaurant, she would know you had a specific dislike or distaste for it. Even if you didn't shake your head, "nah," she would still know how you felt. Why?

Because the two muscle groups you produced are distinct to the disgust family. Your reaction would never occur if you didn't have a strong enough opinion about the restaurant, the staff working there, or the kind of food they serve. Something from the past created that opinion and it's now registering on your face.

We do this constantly without realizing it. Try the exercise below to see if it feels familiar to you.

Exercise

Take a look at photo #44 then try the exercise. Lift your upper lip up towards your nose and shake your head "no." Does it feel familiar?

Try wrinkling your nose slightly and shake your head "no." How about that for familiar?

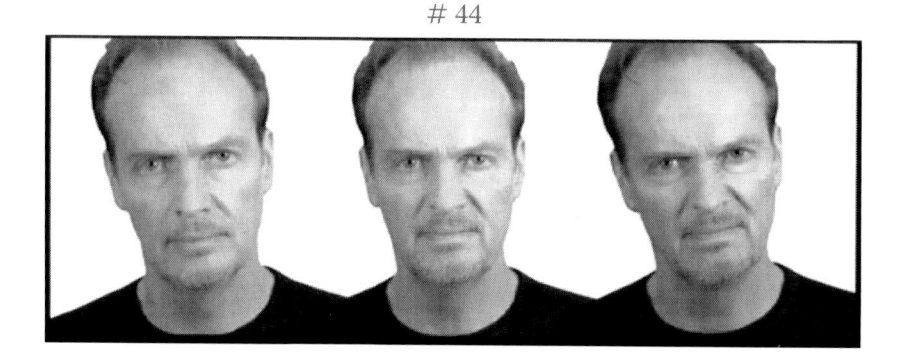

44

I tell my actors, "Your reactions are your thoughts manifested on your face." Understanding how you reveal your own history is the first step in understanding how a character reveals theirs.

Why your thoughts may not appear on your face the way you want

Another reason why the 20% may have difficulty in getting the results the 5% get by "just thinking the thought" is a lack of emotional alignment between what they are feeling and what their faces are revealing.

Even if you have a strong enough thought, there's still no guarantee the camera will pick it up due to how you are wired or how you were raised to express. In the last chapter, we discussed how some actors were born internalizers (they feel intensely but reveal little to nothing) or externalizers (who show everything but have little connection to the emotion). If you fit into either of those groups and haven't made any adjustments, it may explain why your thoughts don't appear on your face as you expect.

If you tend to be an externalizer, the camera will definitely pick up your thoughts; in fact, it will pick up <u>all</u> of your thoughts. Externalizers tend to react to everything. Every thought, whether valid to the scene or not, appears on their face. This over-expressing often confuses the viewer, not knowing what's important and what's not.

If you tend to be more of an internalizer, the camera can't pick up what you're thinking because you're not revealing anything. No matter how many thoughts you have or how intensely these thoughts make you feel, odds are your face will remain blank. It's not your fault; it's just the way you're wired.

Are you modifying your expression?

If you modify your expression in any way because of what you learned through your culture, family or your own personal psychological history, then you may distort the expression of the thought, reveal an inappropriate thought, or reveal nothing at all.

Your thoughts must be in alignment with the character's thoughts and appropriate for what's taking place. For example, if you were brought up not to express fear in public, your fearful thought might be revealed in an angry expression or your irritated thought may appear on your face as a sad expression. If you aren't one of the lucky people who have very little distortion between what you feel and what you reveal, you run the risk of not appearing authentic, genuine or what we most often hear, "real."

If you've been working under the assumption that all you have to do is think a thought and the camera will pick it up, it's time to rethink this belief. A thought, without your opinion, an emotional connection, and an understanding of how you personally express, is a thought the camera cannot see.

As a tool, "just thinking the thought" doesn't supply you with the information you need to understand, create and reveal real, appropriate, recognizable, and repeatable emotional facial expressions, which is how the viewer sees those thoughts.

Just Be Honest

The fourth misconception about on-camera acting and the assumed adjustment the 5% make to get the results they achieve is, "if you create it truthfully, honestly and organically, the reaction will appear on your face appropriately." This tells you not to worry about what your face is doing and just focus on the work, understanding and connecting to the circumstances, the relationships, needs, objectives of your character, and so on. And if this work is done correctly, the belief suggests that the face will take care of itself.

I hate to be redundant, but apparently it does for the 5%. But what about the rest? If it's not happening for you, the only logical conclusion is that there's something missing. Bottom line: if your acting isn't truthful on stage, odds are it's not going to be truthful on-camera either. You'll need more training. But if you're part of the 20% who have the tools to create a believable life on stage, then understanding *why* "just being honest" doesn't translate to your on-camera work will be a huge benefit to you. Again, let's look at what is known about emotions.

Real Life vs. Acting Life

One of the biggest assumptions many actors make about creating an emotional response is that they will respond emotionally to an imaginary situation in the same way they respond to things in real life. But in real life, much of what you feel, the intensity of what you feel, and what you reveal on your face typically happens without your awareness or even consent. In other words, in life, you don't have to be aware of what makes you emotional to be emotional. It just happens.

Let's say you unexpectedly sit on a tack. The first emotion you'll experience is surprise. You don't have to consciously choose surprise. It just happens because the event is unexpected. If you experience pain from the tack, it might trigger some anger for the person who left it there. You don't need to think about what to feel.

If a stray dog starts growling at you and baring his fangs, you don't have to ponder over how you feel. If you perceive harm, immediately your heart starts to beat faster, your breath quickens, and your legs feel warm. If the potential harm increases, you'll feel your eyes widening as your bottom eyelids get tense. Your eyebrows may rise up and pull together. You may even feel the corners of your mouth being pulled back.

These are real responses to real events. All this can happen in a flash of a moment and there is very little you can do about it if the harm is perceived to be real. As we talked about earlier, when an emotion is triggered, emotional facial expressions happen with or without our consent. The most we can do is try to manage or distort them. So, it follows that emotions which are created truthfully, honestly, and organically should be revealed on your face appropriately.

Remember, it's ALL Deception

The fact is acting, especially at an audition, is not "real life." There is no tack for you to sit on or dog threatening to attack you. There's just you, the audition material, and the casting director. You have to create these situations through your own imagination and get the viewer to believe it. That's the deception.

Since you're creating all this from your imagination, without much feedback and not knowing for sure if you're reacting appropriately, you may be unsure as to how surprised or angry you really are about the tack. Just how frightened are you about that dog? Then your brain takes over and starts questioning, is it reading? Is it enough? Is it too much? Are they getting it? And once you're full of those questions, you've left the scene or the commercial and are now in your head. Who knows what might appear on your face at that point?

For most people, experiencing intense emotions and opinions is not a daily occurrence. Yes, we feel things, but how often do you experience *intense* fear, anger, disgust, happiness, or any of the other emotions? How often are you asked to have a real and intense opinion about something you don't think warrants it? This is the life of an actor.

Since our experience of these intense emotions are usually distant memories, when we create them through our imagination they often pale in comparison to what the reality of the situation was. The reason? Emotion can feel so potent sometimes that just creating a little bit of it from our imagination can feel pretty intense, but it often falls quite short of the real thing. And it isn't enough to change our face or compel us to action.

Here's something else to think about. In real life, we have no say about the stimuli we're confronted with or how we feel about it – it just happens. As actors, we are creating the stimuli and have the power to not only modify it, but to actually turn it off.

When it comes to "acting truths," there are many to consider. I'd like to focus on two – the *inner truth* and, just as importantly, the *outer truth*. The inner truth is how you feel; the outer truth is what the viewer sees. So, if you get the adjustment, "just be honest," and you feel that your inner truth is strong, be aware that your outer truth may well be unrecognizable. You need to create and reveal real, recognizable, appropriate facial reactions. No matter how honest you are or how well you execute your craft, if there is a distortion between what you feel and what your face reveals, on-camera acting will be a challenge for you. And the adjustment of "just be honest" will be of little help.

The belief of, "if you create it "honestly and truthfully," it will appear on your face appropriately," is a valid tool for the 5% who are more in alignment with what they feel and what their face reveals. For the rest, you need to fully understand what triggers a real emotion for you, how it feels, and what it compels you to do, as well as what it looks like and feels like on your face. Without that understanding, you haven't yet acquired all the tools you need to be "honest."

What Does this all Mean to the On-camera Actor?

The 4 misconceptions discussed in this chapter are really 2 tools and 2 adjustments.

"Create it truthfully and honestly," and "think real thoughts," are *tools* for working on-camera. And you must invest the time to acquire them. They satisfy and ground the *inner life*. However, you must still be able to manifest those thoughts on your face appropriately, meaning that you're free from any personal distortions that may alter those thoughts or the expression of them.

The adjustments to, "make it smaller," and "bring it through the eyes," are attempts to satisfy the *outer life*. Although they have varying degrees of validity, they're both limited and misleading.

Here's the thing. All the beliefs and adjustments we've covered are attempts to replicate what the 5% does naturally – create real, appropriate, recognizable, and repeatable emotions. But there's a catch. If you're in the 20% and you're trying to replicate what the 5% does, you're trying to duplicate *their* result versus understanding the process *you* need to achieve those emotions.

The good news is that by understanding what the 5% is doing and acquiring new tools that will lead you to the same results as they achieve, you can transform and bring your on-camera acting to a whole new level. Understanding the Language of the Face and learning how to speak it has been the missing link for so many actors I have taught. If you speak the language fluently, it can ultimately take you from the 20% to the desired 5%, with your own unique spin.

Chapter 7

Emotional Alignment: Are You In or Out?

As we look back on our journey so far, we started out in chapter 2 with the idea that acting is an art of deception. And, to successfully achieve deception, you must know what the **truth** feels like in your body, sounds like in your voice and looks and feels like on your face. You must also know what a **lie** feels like in your body, sounds like in your voice and looks and feels like on your face.

In chapter 3, for the first time, we determined the most significant difference between acting for the camera and acting on stage is the use of appropriate facial expressions. Unlike stage acting, the on-camera actor must have the skill to express their most intimate thoughts, feelings and emotions on their face in a way that is appropriate and recognizable by all.

Also, in chapter 3, we established that there's a small percentage of actors who are able to control their facial expression and as a result get the majority of the on-camera work. I've been calling this group, the "5%".

As we looked closer at this 5%, we were able to see the secret to their success wasn't that they were doing things *differently* than the rest, they were actually doing *different* things.

Another group we looked at, I identified as, the 20%. This group has the same potential for on-camera success as the 5%. However, when it comes to creating and controlling what their faces are expressing, they don't appear to be as skilled or consistent as the 5%.

So, as the 20% struggle with their facial communication, the 5% without any additional training, are able to come up with real, recognizable and appropriate facial reactions, do it on demand and repeat the whole process at will.

This process of nonverbal facial communication, I called the Language of the Face. As a reminder, I defined this language as a method of human nonverbal communication that uses specific facial muscles, patterns and movements at various intensities and speed to communicate thought, feeling and emotion.

To better understand the language your face speaks, in chapter 4, we turned our attention to the science of emotion. It was there that we explored the nature and experience of emotions- what they are, what makes us emotional, what emotions feel like in our body, what they compel us to do and what they specifically look like on our face.

It appears that the 5% are more likely to express what they feel in a way that we are hardwired to read it.

In chapter 5, we found the primary reason why the 20% struggled so much with their facial communication was because there was some distortion between what they were feeling and what their face was revealing.

In fact, there were 7 of these distortions that were brought to light, *How you're wired, The culture you were raised in, Family idiosyncrasies, Your own psychology, Inappropriate emotional triggers, How you listen, Your face*. What we found was, the more distortions or the more intense the distortion the greater the challenge of getting your facial message across the way you intend.

So, you could say, what we've discovered so far is that the 5% aren't necessarily better actors, they just have fewer or less intense distortions than the rest. The fewer or less intense the distortion you have the more likely you will express what you feel the way you intend.

Compounding the problem for the 20% is this, if you have any of the distortions I outlined, you need to know they are very insidious, and they don't go away on their own. What I mean by this is, trying to be more honest with your acting or making all your expressions smaller isn't going to solve the problem.

The reason these distortions don't go away on their own is because you can't change something of which you're not aware. In other words, your acting may be considered too big, too small or unrecognizable to others, but to you, it feels right. How you currently express makes sense and feels absolutely appropriate.

> *Warning: If there's a difference between what you feel and what your face reveals booking becomes very difficult. The greater the difference, booking becomes virtually impossible.*

If you are one of the many in the 20%, I know this all sounds like a little bit of a downer, however, I've discovered what you can do to minimize your distortions and learn to speak this nonverbal language organically, the way we were meant to. To do this will take some work on your end. If you're willing to put the work in, I guarantee the reward will be well worth it. At the same time, choosing *not* to put the work in will reap the same rewards as they did in the past.

If there's a difference between what you feel and what your face reveals booking becomes very difficult. The greater the difference, booking becomes virtually impossible. In order to stop the facial communication struggle, you must achieve what I call, "Emotional Alignment."

What is Emotional Alignment?

Emotional Alignment is a phrase I use to establish a relationship between what an actor feels and what they reveal on their face. It's the foundation for speaking the Language of the Face and is based on two factors: inner intensity and outer facial expression.

Inner intensity involves the sensations and impulses you are experiencing internally when an emotion is triggered. You can rate the intensity by noticing changes in your heart rate, breathing, skin temperature, and tension in specific areas of the body, as well as what actions, verbal or physical, you feel compelled to express when you're experiencing the emotion.

Think of the last time you got really angry. How difficult was it to control your breath or heart rate? You may not have even been aware of the changes until you stopped being emotional, but they were there. While experiencing that emotion, you more than likely had the impulse to punish, control, or physically/emotionally hurt the person or thing that triggered the anger in you. Ever say or do something mean that you regretted later? Why'd you do it? Because you were angry.

The outer facial expression is based on how many emotionally related muscle groups appear on your face. As discussed in chapter 3, each of the 7 universal emotions (photo #1) have distinct muscle groups. The more muscle groups that appear on your face, as well as how tense, expanded, contracted, or symmetrical they are, the more intense the expression.

If the inner intensity, without any conscious modification of the expression, is much greater or much less than the outer expression, you are out of emotional alignment.

It's important to note that emotional alignment is <u>not</u> about what *makes* you emotional. Although what you're using as a trigger or the tools you're using to become emotional may be partly responsible for not being in alignment. It's also <u>not</u> about *how long it takes* you to become emotional. Your psychology and internal wiring are chiefly responsible for that. For some, a little conflict sends them over the edge in rage; others have to practically be hit over the head to get any response at all.

Emotional Alignment is more specifically about comparing what you're experiencing internally with how much your face is revealing. Attaining Emotional Alignment is the first step to understanding how you can level the playing field to achieve what comes so naturally to the 5%.

Following are some of the most common symptoms of being out of Emotional Alignment. Check the ones you can say YES to:

- ☐ Can't stop your face from moving.

- No one knows what you're feeling.
- Facial expressions are often unrecognizable.
- Feeling blocked with some or all emotions.
- Every headshot you take looks the same.
- Often told your facial expressions are too big, too small or too messy.
- You have a difficult time adjusting the intensity of the expression.

Anyone of these symptoms can be devastating to your on-camera story telling or your success as an on-camera actor and here is why...

- If you can't **control** what your face is expressing - How are you going to **adjust** it?
- If you don't know **how** you created it - How are you going to **repeat it**?
- If they **don't recognize** what's on your face - How can they **hire** you?
- If you don't have **an awareness** of what you're communicating - How are you going to **change** it?

The biggest challenge on-camera actors face is not that they are out of emotional alignment, but not knowing they're out of emotional alignment.

The Emotion Screen Test (EST)

As an on-camera acting teacher, identifying distortions or finding out how intensely the distortion was influencing a student's emotional facial expressions has always been a frustrating challenge, for both myself as well as the student.

Before I started to study the science of emotions, the idea of distortions in your acting didn't even exist. We were all taught to listen and be guided by the inner truth. However, if a student claim to feel intensely, but showed very little of this intensity on their face, or if they appeared to be showing the emotion without being connected to it, they were often told they were overacting, not honest, indicating and so on. No matter how truthful they felt, they were doing something wrong. Talk about a confusing message. However, that was all about to change.

What I came to realize, the real problem for the actor wasn't about feeling, it was about expressing. They were relying on what they were feeling to determine if they were being truthful or not, no matter what was taking place outwardly. I needed some way to identify the distortion as it occurred and show it to them. In other words, I had to prove to them, feeling something doesn't mean it's going to be expressed the way you feel it.

One day, I asked a student who had just started working with me to create a specific emotion. As he did, I recorded it. Then, right after capturing what I thought was his emotional expression, I asked him to tell me how intensely he thought he felt the emotion. His response was, he felt it quite intensely. With this information we viewed what I recorded. To his surprise, there was very little of this emotion on his face.

When I showed him a photo of what the emotion should look like and compare it to what he did, he was stunned. For the first time, he could actually see that there was a disconnect between what he felt and what his face was revealing. That moment was the birth of what would come to be known as the Emotion Screen Test (EST).

Over time the EST grew in complexity. Now, within a short amount of time, with this simple yet revolutionary test, an actor can determine their own emotion creating and revealing skill level, how effective their acting tools are and what distortions are having the greatest impact on them. Also included is how to read your own face, which is key to branding yourself. (Spoiler Alert) Knowing all this will set you on a path towards Emotional Alignment.

The EST has become such an important part of my emotion training, it's usually the first thing I do with everyone I work with, no matter what their experience. In the next step of our journey together, *Acting Face to Face 2: Emotional Alignment*, I go into the Emotion Screen Test in great detail. I also have an online course that will take you through the whole test step by step. However, for those who can't wait, I want to share a mini version of the emotion screen test here.

I want to assure you, even the mini version of the EST can immediately show you what you are emotionally good at and where you need to put your focus. You'll see what's working and what's not.

With the aid of the mini EST, you'll be able to take that first step towards leveling the playing field by discovering how you personally create and reveal emotion.

If you prefer to wait and do the full version of the Emotion Screen Test, you can. It can be found in book 2 of the Acting

Face to Face Series, Acting Face to Face: Emotional Alignment or you can do the online course. For more information go to *https://www.emotiontrainingcenter.com/store*

Why Do the Emotion Screen Test?

Here's the thing. Prior to reading this book, you may have known or suspected that something wasn't right in the way you were creating or revealing emotion. You can compare this unease to not feeling 100% physically. You know something is wrong, but you can't quite pinpoint what it is. It's not until you visit the doctor and undergo testing that you know the problem. The good news is your doctor can now prescribe a treatment especially for you.

> *The path to changing how you express starts with becoming aware of how you express and why you express the way you do.*

I'm not suggesting that being out of Emotional Alignment is an illness. However, I am saying that being out of Emotional Alignment can keep you from bringing your "A game" to each and every audition. Taking the Emotion Screen Test serves the same purpose as those tests your doctor ran, identifying the challenges preventing you from communicating in the way you intend. Knowing where your personal distortions lie will guide you toward what you need to work on (i.e., tools, triggers and adjustments).

If you are ready to take the Emotion Screen Test, let's do it!

Chapter 8

The Mini Emotion Screen Test

To truly know how far you've traveled, you have to determine where you started. Your journey to Emotional Alignment starts with this mini Emotion Screen Test. Try to think of the Emotion Screen Test as a way of determining where you currently are in creating and revealing emotion. It's the place you can return to at any time to check in on your growth.

To keep this as simple as possible I've broken down the mini EST down into 4 steps:

- Step #1 Create the emotion
- Step #2 Capture the emotion
- Step #3 Select the image
- Step #4 Evaluate the emotion

To execute the Emotion Screen Test, you'll need some type of device to capture each emotion you create. Once all 7 emotions and your static shot have been captured, you will select the ones you want to use for the evaluation process.

What follows is a detailed breakdown for each part of the screen test. I've also provided you with some additional tips and guidelines to help you along the way.

Step 1: Creating the Emotion

- *Create each emotion as richly and as strongly as possible.* At the same time don't push or force it. A good point to shoot for is feeling the emotion fully (i.e. I feel happy, sad, angry, etc.). Don't spend more than a few minutes creating each emotion.

- *Try to avoid modifying what you are feeling in any way.* In other words, don't try to hide or manage the emotion or think bigger or smaller. Think of it as if it is the opening moment in a scene you're filming. The director yells AC-TION, and the camera finds you in whatever emotional state you've selected to work on.

- *Most importantly, focus on the feeling, not what your face is doing!* Your absolute goal is to be experiencing the emotion you have chosen to work on. This is not a face acting test. Focus on connecting to the emotion however you can.

- *Any way you want to prepare for this experience is perfectly fine.* You can move, talk or pull a nose hair if that will work for you. However, once you are ready to capture the moment, all talking and moving needs to come to a stop.

- *Use circumstances from your own life.* Since there is no script, the circumstances you'll need to create each emotional state will be drawn from the story of your life. In other words, under what circumstances would you be angry, sad, surprised and so on.

If you are an actor with reasonable training under your belt, you should have at least some tools to create each of the 7 emotions. If you are not an actor, or don't have the adequate tools for creating an emotion, try to recall a time when you actually felt the emotion you are trying to create. Focus on a time that you were sad or happy or angry. Try to recall what made you feel that way, what it felt like in your body, and allow those feelings to come about again.

Step 2: Capturing Set Up

There are several ways for you to capture the emotion. The easiest ways are to use a:

- Webcam
- Digital still/video camera
- Smart phone

If you use video or a still camera, you may need someone to assist you. Whatever device you use to capture, make sure the lens is set at eye level, and position your face *straight on* to the camera. You shouldn't be looking up, down or from the side.

Framing

The frame should start a few inches below your chin to the top of your forehead. If you have hair that covers your forehead, it's best to move it aside. Most importantly, you'll want to see your full face clearly (See photo# 45).

Taking the shot

When you feel you have created the emotion as strongly as you can, that is the time to roll camera or take several photos. If you are working with someone, set a cue so they will know you are ready for them to start rolling camera or shooting the stills (I simply have my actors give me a thumbs up).

#45

Once framed in, turn your face full to the camera and take a few quick snapshots (or run video or hit capture on your computer). Again, if you are running video, it should only be for a few frames. The camera should find you already in this emotional state, not working to attain it.

> **Special Note on lighting:**
>
> *Whether you are using your webcam, camera or smart phone, make sure there is enough light. Again, you'll want to see yourself clearly, so try to avoid shadows or over-exposing the shot.*

What to Capture

First, start with a static/neutral shot of your face. We want to get you in a listening, nonreactive state. It should feel relaxed, as if you were listening to someone speaking. If at all possible, have someone talk to you as you look directly into the camera. Again, there shouldn't be any reacting to what you hear. Just listen. If it's not possible to get someone to talk to you, just focus on the camera lens and be still for a few moments as you capture.

Next, move on to creating and capturing: **Surprise**, **Fear**, **Anger**, **Disgust**, **Contempt**, **Happy**, and end with **Sadness**.

#46

Rating and Recording the Emotional Experience

1. Rate the intensity of the experience from nothing, slight, moderate, full or extreme. Here is a quick breakdown of each level of intensity for reference.

    - *Nothing*: Nothing simply means you had nothing. For whatever reason, you were unable to connect to this emotion with your current tools or unable to relate to the emotion.

    - *Slight*: The emotion was just beginning or was fleeting.

- *Moderate*: Somewhere between slight and full. You can clearly identify what you were feeling. However, you know you're not quite there yet.
- *Full*: There's no doubt about what you were feeling. You fully experienced the power of the emotion. You felt strong changes in your body and had thoughts associated with that emotion.
- *Extreme*: What you experienced was very intense. You may have had difficulty controlling thoughts or the impulse to do something.

2. Write down any words or images that were used to trigger this emotion. If another emotion other than the one you were creating appears on your face, you will discover why in these notes.

3. Record any sensations you felt after each emotion. These could include changes in breathing, heart rate, tension in the body or tightness in the throat, etc.

4. Note on your evaluation worksheet any desires or impulses that occurred while experiencing this emotion. Did you feel you wanted to do something? For example, to run, hit, yell or turn away?

Download the Emotion Evaluation Worksheets as well as all the other worksheets/Quick Look notes *http://bit.ly/miniestdownload*

Special Note about Surprise:

Surprise is done a little differently than the rest. For the other emotions, we want to capture in that emotional state. Because of the nature of surprise, you will have to be in a neutral state first, then react to the surprising event. It's easier to do if you make the lens of the camera where the surprising event unfolds.

Step #3: THE SELECTION

Once you've captured all 7 emotions and your static shot, it's time to select. If you used video to capture the emotions, the best thing to do is view your content and then select a single frame that best represents the emotion you were trying to create.

If you can, either create a freeze frame or take a screenshot of the frame for each emotion. Put all screenshots or freeze frames into one file so you can easily access them. This would be the same for still photos as well. Printing still photos would be even better.

> **Special Note on Selecting a Frame:**
>
> Pick the strongest frame, but note on your evaluation sheet if the frame chosen wasn't consistent with the other frames. Why? Because if it was the only frame that revealed emotion, it suggests that you were searching for either the emotion or expression of it. It could mean you were either unclear when you arrived at the emotion (a personal distortion at work) or you need to be more specific about the trigger you were using. Either way this emotion will need your attention.

Step #4: The Evaluation

The goal of the evaluation is to see how in and/or out of Emotional Alignment you are. To execute the evaluation, you'll need all the emotion photos you captured, as well as the static shot. Make sure you have the "intensity felt" logged in for each emotion.

The evaluating process will be two fold. You'll start with your static shot and compare it to the emotion you are exploring. Do you see any of that emotion in your static shot? If you do, make sure to note it in your worksheets. Also note what muscle or muscle groups appear to be activated.

By doing this step, you'll be able to determine whether the emotion on your face is the one you've created or merely your static or default face talking. It will also give you insight into why people see you as they do.

Next, match up the photo you took for each emotion with the corresponding emotion. Keep in mind, each photo I've supplied is a macro expression of that emotion, or what I call the "full" emotion. (Just a reminder, the macro expression is the one we usually express if we are feeling the emotion fully, and there is no need to modify it in any way.)

The question you want to ask is: was the intensity in your emotion photo comparable to the intensity "felt" rating? If not, was it less or more than? If so, note it in the worksheets.

The following are some guidelines to determine the level of intensity for your expression. If you rated the emotional experience as:

- **Nothing** – Obviously, if you felt nothing there should be no expression, unless your static face has strong emotional features.
- **Slight** - You should see very little contraction, expansion or tension in any of the muscle groups in that emotion. Whatever you were experiencing will be barely noticeable.

- **Moderate** - Recognizable tension, contraction or expansion activity in at least one muscle group.

- **Full** - All muscle groups necessary to make the emotion recognizable are activated and noticeably contracted, expanded or tensed. In other words, there's no question about what you are experiencing.

- **Extreme** - All muscle groups are expanded, contracted or tensed to the max.

If you're ready, let's start evaluating.

Evaluating Surprise

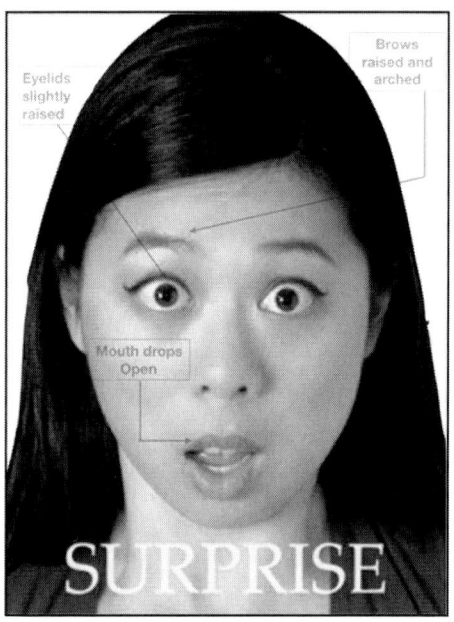

#47

[Image: Woman's face labeled with "Eyelids slightly raised", "Brows raised and arched", "Mouth drops Open", captioned SURPRISE]

Surprise muscle groups evaluation

First look at your static shot and compare it to the Surprise muscle groups. Do you have any of the Surprise muscle groups activated or do any appear to be activated? If so, make a note of which muscle groups are activated.

Second, compare your Surprise shot with the following photos. Do you have one, two, or all three of the muscle groups activated?

As you compare your photo to the ones I supplied, notice if the intensity in your photo is comparable to how you rated it. If not, is it greater or less than how you rated it? Make a note of the level of intensity.

Surprise Brow:

Compare your brows to the ones below (photo #48). Are the eyebrows lifted and arched? Depending on age and/or skin type, you'll see wrinkles across the forehead.

#48

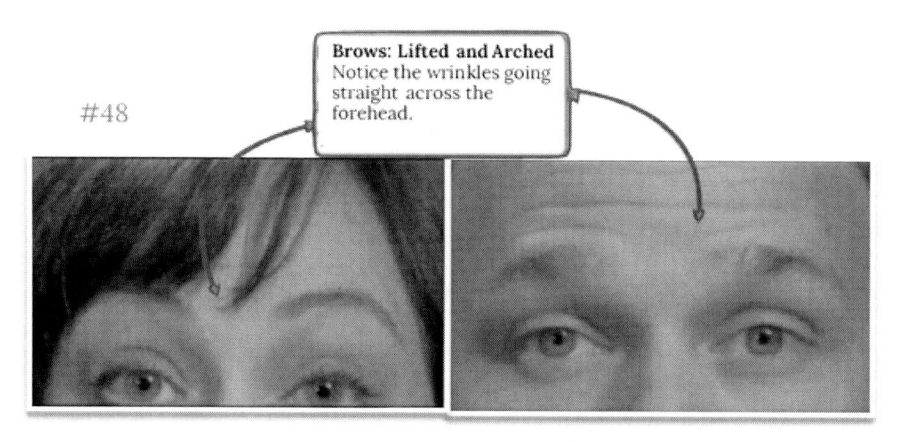

Brows: Lifted and Arched
Notice the wrinkles going straight across the forehead.

Surprise Eyes:

Check below (photo #49). Are your upper eyelids raised, showing the white above the iris? There should be no tension in either the top or bottom lids.

#49

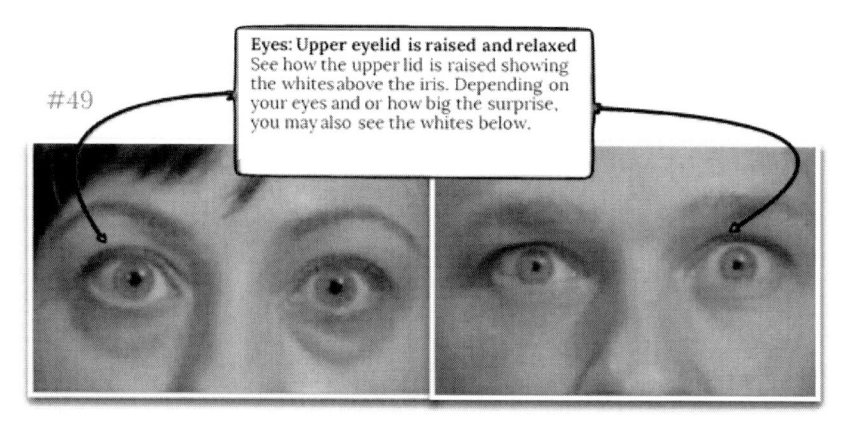

Eyes: Upper eyelid is raised and relaxed
See how the upper lid is raised showing the whites above the iris. Depending on your eyes and or how big the surprise, you may also see the whites below.

Surprise Mouth:

Check below (Photo #50). Is your mouth open and relaxed? Depending on the Surprise, the mouth may only part slightly, or it may literally be jaw-dropping.

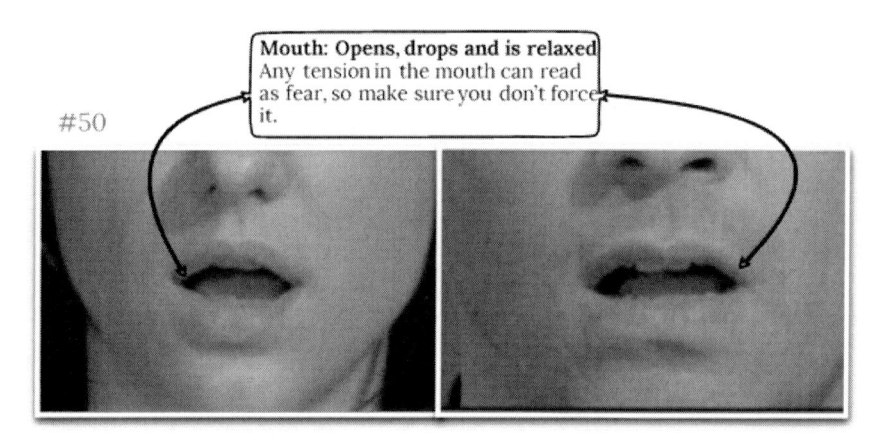

#50

Mouth: Opens, drops and is relaxed
Any tension in the mouth can read as fear, so make sure you don't force it.

Evaluating Fear

#51

Brows slightly raised drawn together

The upper eyelid is raised above the iris and the bottom lid is tensed.

Lips are either tensed slightly and drawn back.

FEAR

Fear muscle groups evaluation

First look at your static shot and compare it to the Fear muscle groups. Are any of the muscle groups of Fear activated or do any appear to be activated? If so, make a note of which muscle groups are activated.

Second, compare your Fear shot with the following photos. Do you have one, two, or all three of the muscle groups activated?

As you compare your photo to the ones I supplied, notice if the intensity in your photo is comparable to how you rated it. If not, is it greater or less than how you rated it? Make a note of the level of intensity.

Fear Brow:

Check below (photo #52) Are your eyebrows lifted and drawn together? Depending on age and/or skin type you should see wrinkles in the center of the forehead.

Brows: Raised and drawn together
Notice the wrinkles in the center of the forehead.

#52

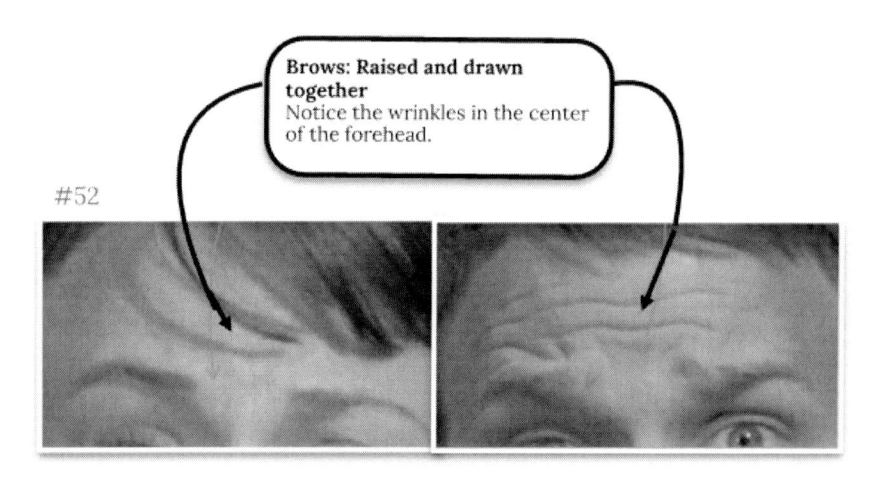

Fear Eyes:

Check below (photo #53) to see if the upper eyelids are raised/the lower eyelids are tensed.

Eyes: Upper lid is raised- bottom lid is tense.

#53

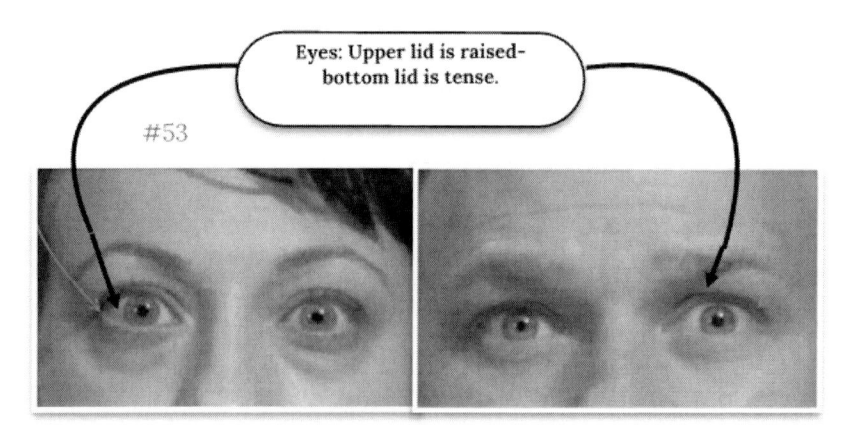

Fear Mouth:

Check below (photo #54) to see if your lips are tensed or stretched back or down.

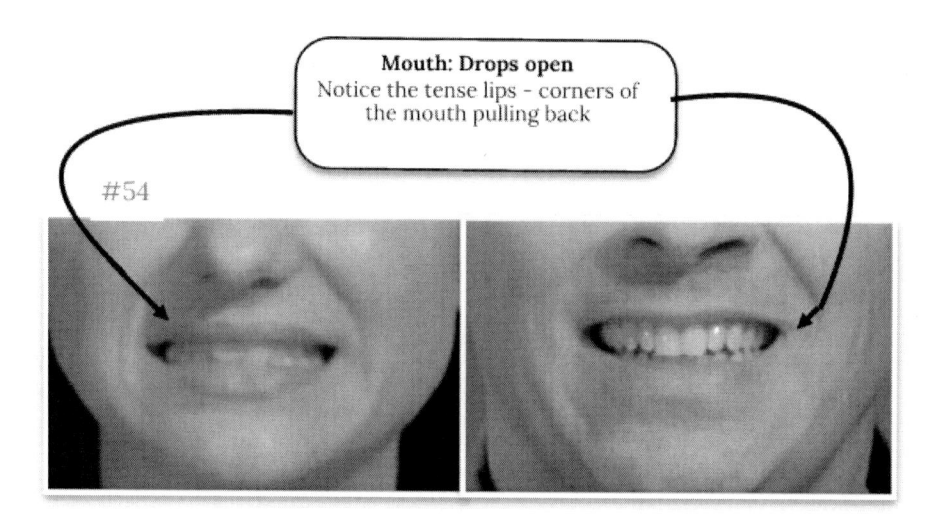

Mouth: Drops open
Notice the tense lips - corners of the mouth pulling back

#54

Evaluating Anger

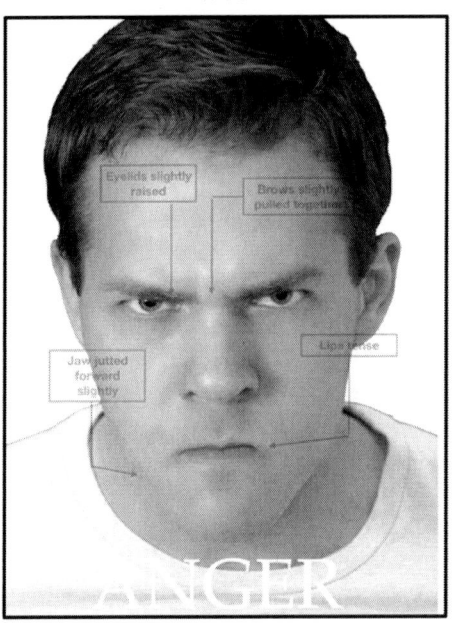

#55

[Photo labels: Eyelids slightly raised; Brows slightly pulled together; Jaw jutted forward slightly; Lips tense — ANGER]

Anger muscle groups evaluation

First look at your static shot and compare it to the Anger muscle groups. Do you have any of the muscle groups of Anger activated or do any appear to be activated? If so, make a note of which muscle groups are activated.

Second, compare your Anger shot with the following photos. Do you have one, two, or all three of the muscle groups activated? As you compare your photo to the ones I supplied, notice if the intensity in your photo is comparable to how you rated it. If not, is it greater or less than how you rated it? Make a note of the level of intensity.

ACTING: FACE TO FACE

Special Note:

To really be sure you're feeling and revealing full Anger, you'll need to activate all 3 muscle groups. If you see only 1 or 2, you are either controlling your Anger, or on the way to getting angry.

Anger Brow: Check below (photo #56) Are your eyebrows pulled down and drawn together? Can you see the vertical lines on your brow?

#56

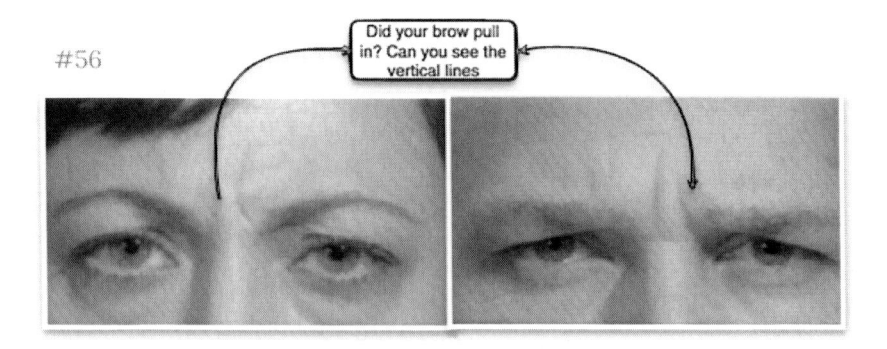

Did your brow pull in? Can you see the vertical lines

Anger Eyes:

Check below (photo #57) Are the upper eyelids raised? Is there tension in the lower lid?

#57

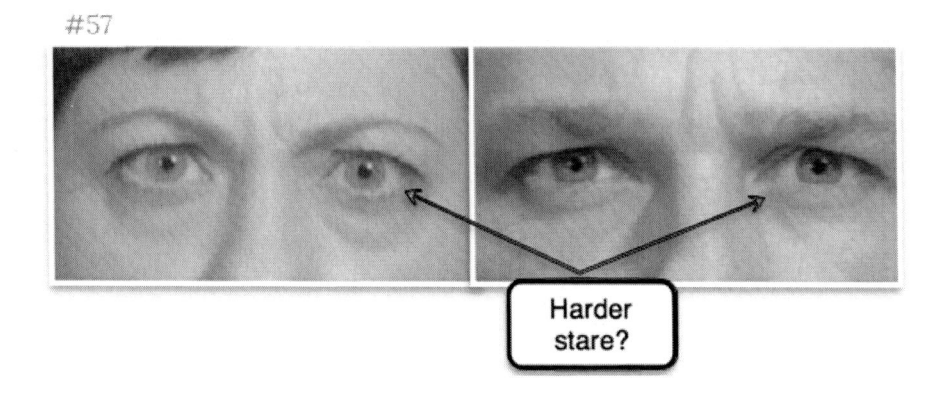

Harder stare?

153

Anger Mouth:

Check below (photo # 58) Are your lips tensed? Jaw jutting forward?

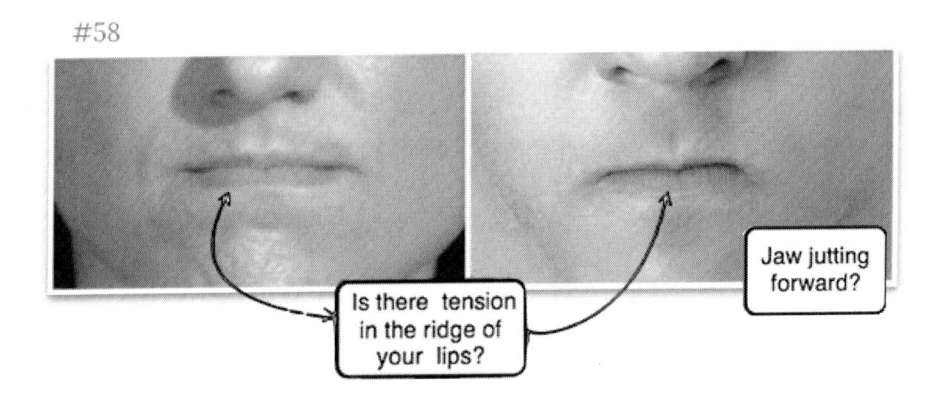

#58

Is there tension in the ridge of your lips?

Jaw jutting forward?

Evaluating Disgust

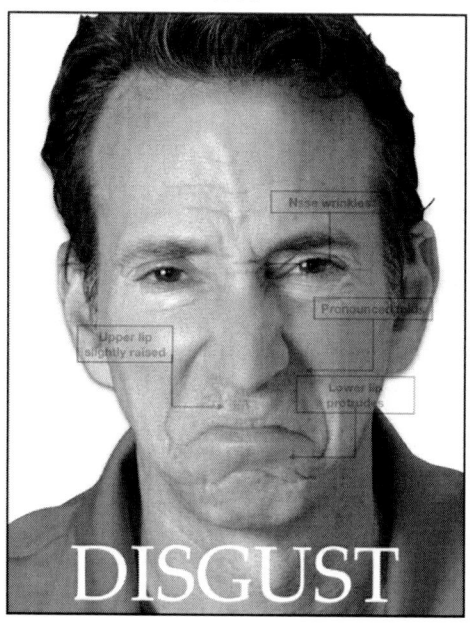

#59

DISGUST

- Nose wrinkles
- Pronounced folds
- Upper lip slightly raised
- Lower lip protrudes

Disgust muscle groups evaluation

First look at your static shot and compare it to the Disgust muscle groups. Are any of the Disgust muscle groups activated or do any appear to be activated? If so, make a note of which muscle groups are activated.

Second, compare your Disgust shot with the following photos. Do you have one or both muscle groups activated?

As you compare your photo to the ones I supplied, notice if the intensity in your photo is comparable to how you rated it. If not, is it greater or less than how you rated it? Make a note of the level of intensity.

Disgust Mouth:

Check below (photo #60) Is your upper lip raised toward your nose? Do you see more intense folds on the side of your nose?

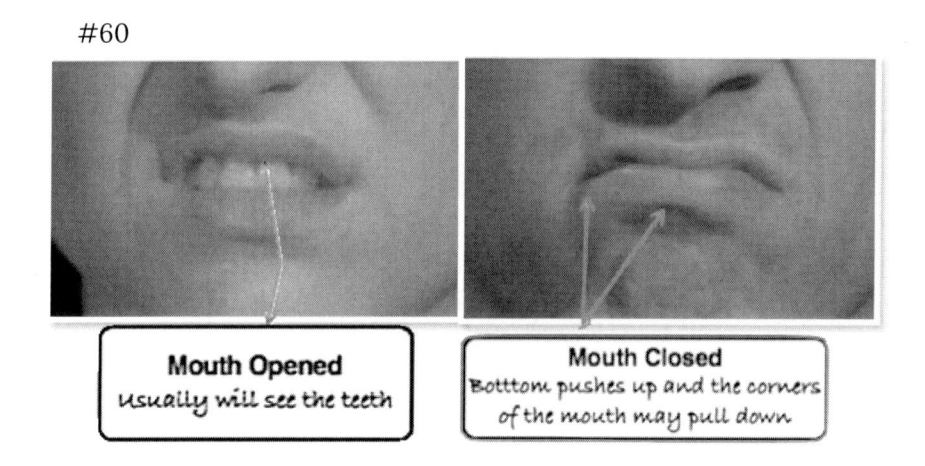

#60

Mouth Opened
usually will see the teeth

Mouth Closed
Botttom pushes up and the corners of the mouth may pull down

Disgust Nose:

Check below (photo #61) Can you see the nose wrinkled? If the nose wrinkles enough, it will pull the brow down. The cheeks will also raise up, which in turn narrows the eyes. This is why Disgust is often misread as Anger.

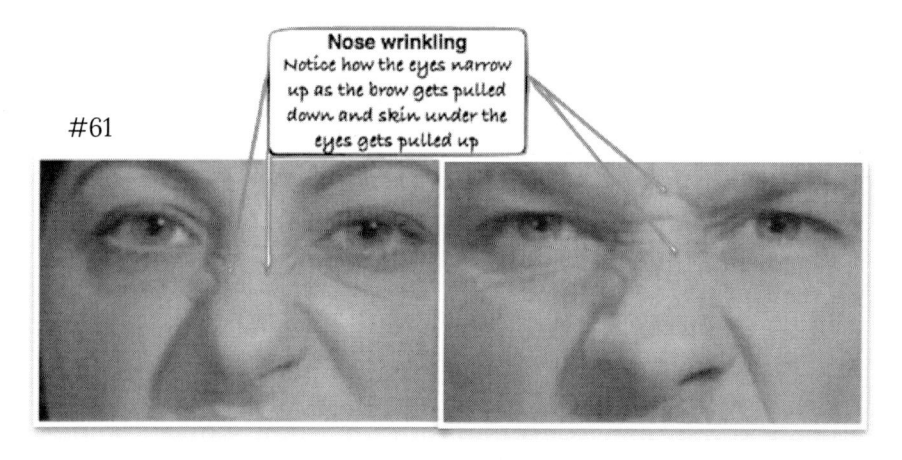

#61

Nose wrinkling
Notice how the eyes narrow up as the brow gets pulled down and skin under the eyes gets pulled up

Evaluating Contempt

#62

Contempt muscle groups evaluation

First look at your static shot and compare it to the contempt muscle group. Do you have the muscle groups of contempt activated or does it appear to be activated? If so, make a note.

Second, compare your Contempt shot with the following photo. Do you see any clamping or lifting of the lip corner?

As you compare your photo to the one I supplied, notice if the intensity in your photo is comparable to how you rated it. If not, is it greater or less than how you rated it? Make a note of the level of intensity.

Contempt Mouth:

Check below (Photo #63) Are the lips on the corner of one side of your mouth pressing together? You should see a little dimple. Is the same corner lifting? It doesn't matter if it's on the left or the right side.

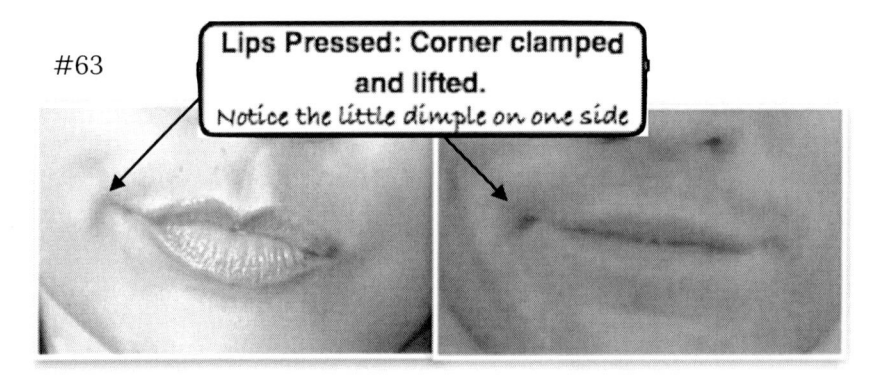

#63

Lips Pressed: Corner clamped and lifted.
Notice the little dimple on one side

Evaluating Happy

#64

Wrinkles form below the eye and corners.

raised cheeks

Corners are drawn back and up.

HAPPY

Happy muscle groups evaluation

First, look at your static shot and compare it to the Happy muscle groups. Does your face have any of the Happy muscle groups activated or do any appear to be activated? If so, make a note of which muscle groups are activated.

Second, compare your Happy shot with the following photos. Do you have all the same muscle groups activated?

The eyes naturally narrow and crow's feet appear if your smile is really big. If this is the case, determine whether you had a specific trigger or if you just put on a smiley face. Is the intensity comparable to how you rated it? If not, is it greater

JOHN SUDOL

or less than how you rated it? Make a note of the level of intensity.

Happy Eyes:

Check below (Photo #65). Are your cheeks raised up, narrowing the eyes? Are there crow's feet?

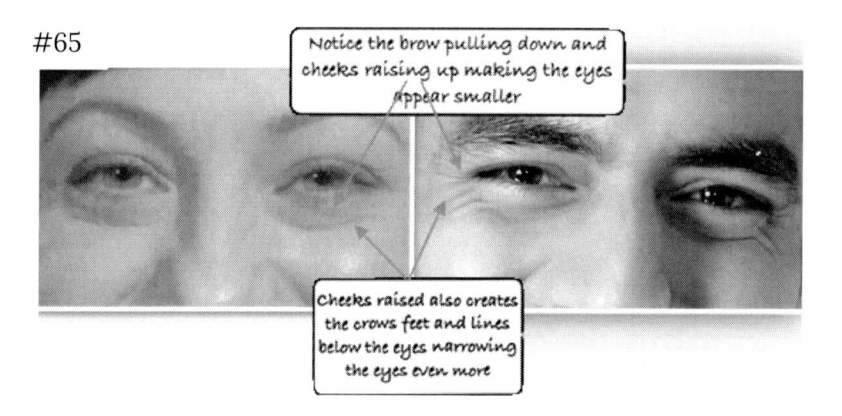

#65

Notice the brow pulling down and cheeks raising up making the eyes appear smaller

Cheeks raised also creates the crows feet and lines below the eyes narrowing the eyes even more

Happy Mouth:

Check below (photo # 66) Are the corners of your mouth back and up? Do you see more intense folds on the side of your nose?

#66

Notice how deep the folds are from the corners being pulled back.

160

Evaluating Sad

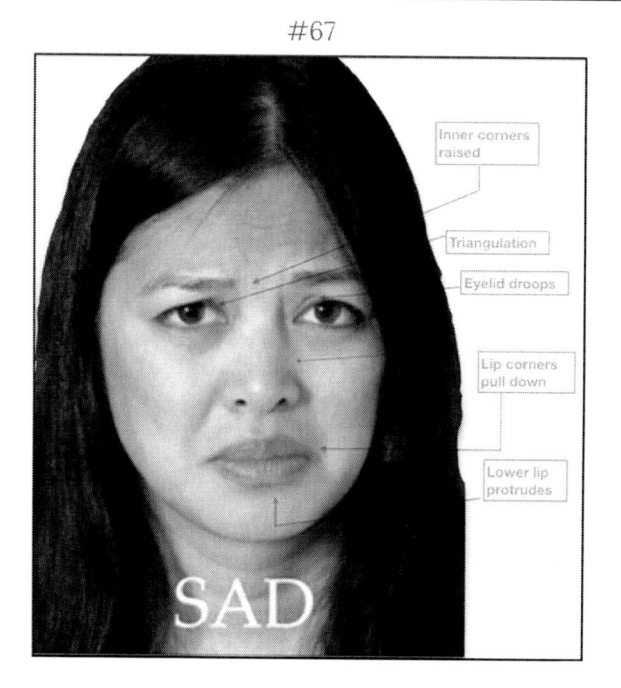

#67

Image labels: Inner corners raised; Triangulation; Eyelid droops; Lip corners pull down; Lower lip protrudes. SAD

Sad muscle groups evaluation

First, look at your static shot and compare it to the Sad muscle groups. Do you have any of the muscle groups of Sad activated? If so, make a note of which muscle groups are activated.

Second, compare your Sad shot with the following photos. Are you utilizing one or both of the Sad muscle groups? Although Sad can be felt and read with just one muscle group, Full Sad needs activity in both muscle groups.

As you compare your photo to those I supplied, notice if the intensity in your photo is comparable to how you rated it? If not, is it greater or less than how you rated it?

Sad Brow and Eyes:

Check below (Photo #68). Are your eyebrows slightly pulled together and the inner portion of the brows raised? Can you see a triangulation in the corner of the eye? If your brows are naturally high you may not see any triangulation.

#68

Drooping Eyelids

Did your brows pull in and corners raise up?

Sad Mouth:

Check below (photo # 69) Are the corners of your mouth pulling downward? Does your bottom lip slightly protrude? Can you see a dimple on your chin?

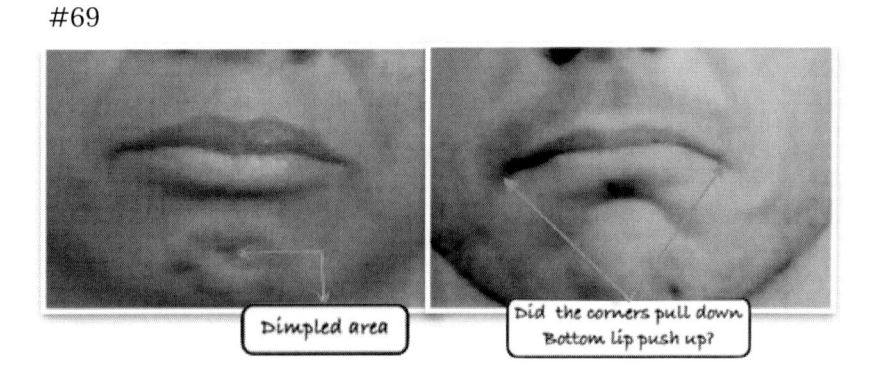

#69

Dimpled area

Did the corners pull down Bottom lip push up?

Step 5: The Assessment

This is the final step of the Mini Emotion Screen Test. If you captured your emotion and did the evaluation, I want to congratulate you. I know it's a lot of work. I'm sure at this point you want to know, what does it all mean? Well, that's the purpose of the assessment.

For this step, it would be a good idea to have your photos and your evaluation worksheets handy. If you've rated the level of intensity felt and intensity revealed for each emotion you captured on your worksheets, you are going to look and see if there are any substantial or consistent distortions. These distortions are the hardest for you to detect on your own and, potentially the most detrimental to your on-camera acting success.

Keep in mind, the purpose of the assessment process is to make you think about how you create and express emotion. There are many reasons why you might be out of alignment. Without knowing you personally, I can only guess. However, based on my previous work with actors, I know the reasons that most often prevented them from expressing what they intended. Reasons for being out of alignment have been commonly found in either the tools, triggers or one of the distortions I've already discussed.

Tools

A *skilled* actor has the tools to create an emotional experience from imagination, a past experience or a combination of both. If you find you don't have the right tools (or any tools), what does this mean for you? Well, it could mean a couple of things. On the one hand, the answer may be simple -- acquire the tools you need, and all should be good. On the other hand, after acquiring your tools (which we'll explore in the following chapters), you may want to retake the screen test and evaluation. I say this because, since you didn't have the tools to create the emotion during the screen test, you can't be absolutely sure you don't have any of the personal distortions. That being said, as you move on to the alignment process and work it, you should be able to identify and overcome any challenges you discover.

Triggers

To evoke an emotional state, your triggers must be specific and important to you. If neither specific nor important, at best you will evoke a lesser or different emotional state, and at worst, no emotion at all.

If your challenges lie mostly in the triggers you were using, your first step is to reevaluate and readjust those triggers. For example, you may now realize your Sadness trigger actually made you Angry, so changing the trigger might be the only adjustment you need. However, if that's not the case, you may need to delve deeper to find what is really important to you. I suggest you continue to explore the chapters on emotions and tap further into your imagination in order to find out what it really takes to make something important enough for you to become emotional.

Personal Distortions

If it seems that your challenges stem from personal distortions, you may want to dig deeper into your own psychology, exploring how you were raised, the people who influenced you and the culture in which you grew up. I also suggest examining your relationship with any emotion(s) you have difficulty expressing.

If you naturally tend to express more (or less) than you actually feel, you'll need to consciously monitor the expression until you build a new relationship with it and its sensations. The example I like to give for this is taking singing lessons. Let's face it, not all of us were born with a pitch-perfect voice. If you went to a singing teacher and sang a song with a few flat notes, the teacher would give you adjustments to hit the notes correctly. They may suggest you sing over the note, which translates into going a little higher than you think and feel the note would be. You may be a little apprehensive in doing this, as doing so could make you seem foolish, or maybe it just feels wrong or unnatural. However, when you do it and hear it, it sounds right.

It will take time before singing over the note feels natural to you. It's the same with emotional expression. However, with time and practice, the whole process will feel more natural to you.

Distortion Indicators

There are Six *Distortion Indicators* for which to look. As you look through each of your emotion photos, you'll be checking to see if the emotions were:

- *Similar to one another*
- *Consistently low intensity*
- *Consistently high reveal, low intensity*
- *Consistently high intensity, low-to-no reveal*
- *Lacked clarity*
- *Blended with other emotional messages.*

Each of these distortion indicators will not only give you clues about where your challenges lie, but will also hint at what you need to examine to achieve Emotional Alignment.

The following is a brief description of each Distortion Indicator and its meaning. At the end of this chapter is a quick look sheet for your reference.

Similar Expression

If you found that most of your expressions were similar, then this may indicate that either your tools aren't specific enough, or you're guessing at what the expression would be.

If you consistently rated the intensity level as moderate to full, it may mean that you have learned to change the expression deliberately. In other words, if a little feeling is stimulated, it leads you to a familiar expression that is more acceptable to express. It can be considered your "go-to" expression; no matter what you feel you tend to express it the same way.

Consistent low-level of intensity

If you found that you rated most of your expressions as none to slight, the first place to look is your tools and triggers. If they were slight to moderate, and the expression matched up, then this is a good indication that you understand the emotions. However, either your tools aren't specific enough to connect you to your triggers long enough, or your triggers aren't hot enough to take you where you want to go.

High reveal, low intensity

If you found that your face revealed most of the emotions fully, yet you had little inner intensity, OR if the expression was forced or exaggerated, it could mean that you just bypassed tools and triggers completely and went right for the expression.

If you know you don't have the tools, but you know what emotions feel like on your face and can mimic them, this is one thing. If you do have tools and can connect to triggers, but you still don't get much inner intensity, the distortion could be in how you are wired to express. You may need more stimuli to get the sensations and impulses that accompany the emotion.

Something else to consider is that somewhere in life you made an expression shift. What I mean by that is, you were originally wired to be an internalizer. At some point you decided it wasn't working for you, so you learned how to express/show emotion in a way that everyone recognized. To actually feel an emotion at the same degree in which you are now expressing would be way too intense, and this could explain the high reveal, low intensity problem you now face.

High intensity, low-to-no reveal

If you consistently came up with no expression or very slight expression, yet felt it intensely, the challenge could lie in ineffective tools and/or triggers. It could also mean that you have learned not to express what you feel, or it's just how you are wired to express. That means, for you, a little feels like a lot. To express more would feel like you are over-acting. In order to express more, you might have learned to turn off the feeling and just go for what you think someone wants you to show.

Lack of Clarity

An expression that is unclear or unrecognizable can easily be traced back to your tools or triggers. It could also be related to how you learned to express that emotion. Does the expression look like someone you know? Is that how Mom looks when she's happy or Dad looks when he's mad? If so, perhaps you've learned over time how to manage the intensity of the emotion, and the expression was distorted as well.

Blended With Other Emotions

If two or more emotional messages consistently appear on your face, the first place to look is your static shot. Look at your static shot. Does it already have the appearance of emotion etched on it? If so, there's a good chance some of the other emotions will show more than the message being sent. If there is already Sadness on your face, it may color your Happy, Fear or Anger expression. Another place to look is your triggers. As I've already stated, if you have more than one feeling about an experience, the strongest one will appear on your face, hence giving you a blend. For example, you are Angry because your lover left you and at the same time Sad because of the loss of the relationship. You got both messages -- Sad and Angry.

Below is a quick look Assessment and Distortion chart. Check the boxes you feel apply to you. You can use this one or download one here – *http://bit.ly/miniestdownload*

Quick Look Assessment and Distortion Chart			
Assessment Check what Applies	**Tools**	**Triggers**	**Personal Distortion**
Most expressions appear similar			
Consistent low Intensity			
High reveal low intensity			
High intensity-none to low expression			
Lack of clarity			
Conflicting or blends of expression			

What Does this all Mean to the On-camera Actor?

If after taking my mini Emotion Screen Test, you found that you are indeed out of alignment with some or all of the emotions, don't let it alarm you.

So often in the past, after doing the EST, I've seen actors blame or start judging themselves harshly because the internal life they were experiencing didn't match up with what they were expressing. If you find that you are doing the same, my best advice to you is to keep your eye on the carrot. The goal is to not look back, but forward. The more you can refrain from judgment or any other form of unproductive criticism, the more you will open yourself up to what can be, and the better off you will be.

As I said earlier, the first step to learning to speak the Language of the Face and become the on-camera storyteller you desire is to achieve Emotional Alignment. In the next chapter, I will lay out just what you need to do to minimize your distortions and create a balance between what you feel and the facial messages you wish to send.

Chapter 9

Emotional Alignment: Your Path to On-Camera Success

You may be at a point now where you realize what you've been doing in your auditions, on the set or headshots hasn't been working for you or hasn't been working consistently enough. If your acting is constantly too big too small or you have trouble adjusting it, if what you feel is consistently different than what you reveal, then you know something has to change.

The main reason it has to change is because what it means to be an on-camera storyteller today is changing. Auditions are changing. Whether you are actually going in person for an audition, self-taping or you're doing a live zoom audition, it's changing. What's expected from you on the set is also changing.

Casting is expecting more from you and so is your director. The bottom line is, you're expected to be good with emotional and non-emotional facial expressions. You're expected to have control over how your face expresses your thoughts, feelings and emotions and if you're not, you will be at a serious disadvantage over those who can. A big part of how good you are with your facial communication will depend on how close to emotional alignment you are. Here's why:

When you are in emotional alignment:

- Your verbal, physical and facial emotional communications are clear, recognizable and much easier to adjust as needed.
- Your actions and reactions are more apt to be appropriate and properly motivated.
- You don't have to guess what or how much you're revealing.
- You are more apt to prepare appropriately for the character's emotional state. If you prepare appropriately, you are less likely to rely on the words or physicalization to achieve the emotion you desire.
- Modifying what you are feeling and expressing becomes much more reliable.

When you're *not* in emotional alignment:

- You're constantly guessing at what you're revealing.
- You have to rely on words and physical actions to generate and communicate what you feel.
- You are often confused by the feedback you get from others who are viewing you.
- You have trouble with adjusting what you are revealing.

The 4 steps to Emotional Alignment

Here's the thing about emotional facial expression you need to know — the playing field is not level. Some actors were actually born and/or raised to be better at facial communication. They tend to naturally be in emotional alignment. However, the times have changed. With the science of emotions to guide us, we can now level the playing field.

After over 20 years of research, trial and error and working with thousands of actors, I have finally found a reliable path to emotional alignment. I believe, if you dedicate yourself to executing the following steps, you can overcome many of the on-camera challenges that you are faced with and become the on-camera storyteller you know you are capable of being.

The following four steps are critical in bringing about emotional alignment.

1. *Identify how you create and reveal emotion*
2. *Master the Inner Truth*
3. *Master the Outer Truth*
4. Master combining the Inner and Outer Truth

Breaking down the steps to Emotional Alignment

To prepare you for the next stage of our journey, we'll go deeper into each step of the alignment process. I would like to cover the steps as well as some action steps you can take now to prepare for the Emotional Alignment process.

Step 1: Identify how you create and reveal emotion/Emotion Screen Test

This first step is all about exploring how you personally create and express emotion on your face in order to detect and ultimately eliminate any distortions. In other words, it's about where you are right now and what feels right to you. Here's the thing. If you are a mystery to yourself, it's hard to make changes.

> **Step 1** *brings focus to any adjustment you'll need to make in your emotional facial communications.*

For anyone working in front of the camera, this means identifying your emotion creating and revealing strengths and weaknesses. If you're just starting out or you're stuck in your progress, identifying your strengths and your weaknesses can do a number of things for you.

*Knowing your strength*s validates what you're doing right and aids in building self-trust and confidence. *Identifying your weaknesses* acts like a checklist telling you what you need to work on, what adjustments need to be made and where you need to put your focus.

When you are unaware of your strengths or weaknesses, everything seems to be hit or miss. You never really know why one moment you're nailing it and the next you're not.

I believe the Emotion Screen Test is one of the most important first steps you can take and that's why I shared the mini version with you in chapter 8. Although the mini EST revealed a lot about how you create and reveal emotion, the one we'll be doing in book 2 or in the online course will be much more detailed.

In the full EST, we'll be going much deeper into your static face and what it may be saying to others without your knowledge or possible consent. I'll also be going over how you can use it to define your brand.

Whether you've done the mini EST or not, the Emotion Screen Test is your starting place. It's something you can always come back to check in on your progress. Once you know what adjustments you need to make and how to make them, you're on your way to emotional alignment.

> **Action Step #1**: *Go back to chapter 5 and look over the 7 distortions and see which one(s) applies to you. Take a little time to explore and write out how any of the distortions have impacted your emotional expression.*

Step 2: Mastering the Inner Truth

This second step is about gaining a greater understanding of emotions – what they are, how they're triggered, what they feel like, what they compel you to say or do and what they feel and look like on your face. It's also the step where your emotional alignment begins.

> **Step 2** *lays the foundation for not only interpreting sides, copy, and directions, but heightens your awareness of inner intensity.*

Triggers

Understanding what triggers an emotional response in you or your character and why is important for you to know because when you are able to pinpoint the triggers in material you can determine the exact point when emotional response begins and at what intensity. Conversely, failing to pinpoint the trigger often leads to over-acting, pushing too hard or not appearing as though you are relating to the problem.

Sensations

Understanding the sensations produced by an emotion gives you the physical clues as to where you are in the experience of the emotion. Knowing what sensations to look for ensures you are not only experiencing the emotion that you intend at the appropriate inner intensity, but are emotionally alive even when you are not speaking.

Impulses

Understanding impulses produced by an emotion will guide you to what action(s) are appropriate to take. Impulses are what inspire behavior. However, not knowing how to behave is the quickest way to shut your instrument down. When you understand what your character feels you also know what they want to do.

Understanding these three interdependent parts of emotion: Triggers, Sensations and Impulses and their variations is what is going to help you to connect, interpret and build your inner truth. They are the key to creating a three dimensional character.

As an on-camera storyteller, expanding your understanding of emotions will give you greater insights to not only what your character feels but why they feel it and what they want to do because of what they are feeling. This is what's going to help you make more creative and credible choices. It's also going to help you to become more specific and precise about evoking an emotional state.

Here's the thing. Being *emotionally free* is a wonderful feeling, however without being *emotionally precise*, the results are often more self-serving than storytelling. Understanding the complex world of emotions is your first step to becoming emotionally precise.

Something else to think about-

- If you know about the three interdependent parts of emotion, you have the tools to interpret all the emotions your character is feeling and why they are feeling them.
- If you know what your character is feeling, you know how to react appropriately.
- If you know what the sensations and impulses produced by the emotions feel like when you create them, you know where you are in the experience of the emotion.

Action Step #2: *Pay attention to when you get emotional - A good idea would be to keep an emotion journal. Pay special attention and note any specific sensations, impulses or changes in thoughts. If possible, sneak a peek at your own face.*

Step 3: Master the Outer Truth

This step is all about gaining control over the individual emotional facial muscle groups and activating them at will. This is ultimately what the viewer sees and interprets.

As we have learned, you can have a strong connection to the inner truth without any outward expression. This step is what ensures that your inner message gets through to the viewer the way you intend.

Step 3 not only prepares you to communicate your thoughts, feelings, and emotions in a recognizable way, but also brings a heightened awareness to outer expression.

Mastering the outer expression or outer truth starts with learning to locate, isolate an organically activate each of the individual facial muscles and muscle groups involved in each of the 7 universal emotions with the correct timing, intensity and duration (see chapter 4).

A big part of the emotional alignment process will be learning what emotions and combinations of emotions at various levels of intensity look and feel like on your face and how to activate each one of them on demand.

Controlling the emotional facial muscle groups opens the door to expressing all the lower intensity or more subtle emotions as well. It will also give you control over the level of intensity of the expression. For example, the more muscle groups activated along with more tension, contraction or lifting of the muscle groups, the bigger the expression. Conversely, the less muscle groups, tension, lifting or contraction, the smaller, more subtle the expression.

The benefits that spring from this step are massive. Think about it. With one subtle facial muscle movement, you have the potential of revealing history, discovery, uncertainty, interest or pleasure. You can also define relationships or send clear messages about your intentions. It's the facial movement or expressions that will provide the subtext to the words you speak.

Learning what emotions look and feel like on your face is how you'll know you are communicating the message you intend truthfully. It will also ensure that you are expressing it at the appropriate intensity.

> **Action Step #3**: *Start having more of awareness of the face of others. Notice when other people are experiencing strong opinions, feelings or emotion. Try to memorize their face or mold yours to theirs, then go back to chapter 3 and see what emotion or emotions match up.*

Step 4: Combining the Inner and Outer Truth

This fourth step is about learning to put it all together. To combine the inner and outer truth you must have a clear path from stimulus to response. And, as you travel down this path you must make any necessary adjustments to compensate for any personal distortions you may have found when you did the emotion screen test.

The path to evoking a genuine emotional response looks like this. First, you must direct your focus in such a way that it comes into contact with something meaningful enough to you that it produces changes in thought and sensations. These internal changes then must be guided outward, so they appear on your face in a real, recognizable and appropriate way with the correct timing, intensity and duration.

To combine the inner and outer truth to you need to answer the following 3 questions: What am I reacting to? Why am I reacting to it? How am I reacting to it? What and why you react to something connects you to the inner truth, to what you feel and think. How you react, meaning what emotional facial muscles come into play connects you to the outer truth.

It's what the viewer sees and interprets. It's the answering of these 3 questions and then executing the answers accordingly is what lays the foundation for a truthful response.

> *Step 4 teaches you a process that will make your emotional response believable and repeatable. Drilling this step will ensure you'll have the correct timing, intensity, and duration.*

To ensure that your connection to the imaginary stimuli is specific enough, you'll need to gain the tools to create outside of your head. In my classes, online course and in book 2, one of the tools we use to create emotional responses to imaginary stimuli are sensory exercises.

The sensory exercises I use are simple, yet effective and not exactly done in the traditional way.

Like traditional sense memory exercises, we do relive sensations experienced though our five senses. However, whereas traditional sense memory exercises are used for exploration, our purpose will be different. We will use the sensations to act as an anchor to what we are reacting to. This might be to a specific sound, touch taste, a sight or smell. This connection to real sensation produced through our imagination ensures that we really interact with the stimuli and respond at the correct timing.

> **Action Step#4**: *Bring more awareness to your emotion building process. Notice when it's working for you and more importantly when it fails you. For example, you used a trigger that didn't produce the response you in-*

tended or maybe you consistently lose emotional intensity, i.e., you reach an emotional state, but for one reason or another it quickly dissipates.

The Payoff

By getting into Emotional Alignment, you are on your way to becoming a more dynamic and effective on-camera storyteller. Once you're in Emotional Alignment and begin speaking the Language of the Face, working in front of the camera will begin to change in significant positive ways, such as:

- Newfound confidence in knowing how to trigger any emotion or combination of emotions organically.

- Heightened awareness of just where you are in the experience and intensity of that emotion, which is required for your character work.

- A clearer understanding of what to do when casting requests that you make your reaction bigger or smaller.

- How to take and make adjustments on demand when in high stress-producing auditions.

- How to create headshots that really show who you are and what you do best, because who you are can be defined emotionally. Once you know who you are from an emotional standpoint, you'll be able to create what you choose to display on your face consciously.

- A change in how people "read" you. If what's on your static face isn't in alignment with how you see yourself or how you want others to see you, you will have the awareness of it and the tools to adjust it. However, if what's on your static face is in alignment with who you are, you will gain an awareness of what it is and how to use it in a way that works for you.

Overall, you'll be able to trade in your old truth barometer that hasn't been working that well for you for a new one that is far more accurate and reliable.

Most importantly, when you get into emotional alignment, you will have the tools to create complex human emotion and reveal it on your face in a real, recognizable, and appropriate way, from the most subtle to the extreme, and make it all look effortless.

The road from the 20% to the 5% relies upon how dedicated you are in gaining the tools and making any necessary changes. Understanding this process has been extremely revealing for the actors I've worked with around the world. Many have gone on to say that this work has not only been career-changing, but life-altering as well.

It has been my passion and my mission to make this work available to all those seeking an alternative to what has historically been taught, as well as provide answers for the challenges that many are experiencing. My goal is to give courage and confidence to the many actors, as well as others in the emotional communications business, who are relentless and driven to attain their dreams.

By putting the information you've learned into action, the whole process will become second nature. The only way to do that is to practice, practice, practice.

> *I believe, wholeheartedly, if you have the tools, determination and dedication – you **will** succeed.*

About the Author

Although John Sudol has been teaching acting for over 30 years, there's much more to John's story. During that time, he has worked successfully as an actor as well as a director. He was the Artistic Director and resident playwright of the 65th Street Theater in Seattle and the Co-Founder of Performing Actor's Studio in Los Angeles.

During his Seattle days, in addition to running a theater and teaching, John also co-founded Casting Northwest, which cast numerous national and regional commercials, theatrical production, features, voiceovers and led several talent searches in the Northwest for ABC.

Returning to LA, John continued casting, working as a session director for some of the busiest casting directors in town while simultaneously acting, teaching and working as a screenwriter and story editor. But it was the years he spent in casting that most inspired his work in The Language of the Face. He realized that the hardest thing for the majority of actors to do was to come up with a real, recognizable reaction on demand. All this culminated in John writing two bestselling books *Acting: Face to Face* (2013) and *Acting: Face to Face 2* (2015). These two books continue to sell globally and have resulted in John being known as the "Go-To Emotion Specialist."

John has dedicated the bulk of his career to studying and understanding emotions and how that applies to artistic expression. He's done this by studying the work of leading scientific researchers in the field of emotions. This study has made him an expert in not only how we do express emotion, but the various reasons that some people may actually fail to do so.

Developing the Language of the Face and the classes that go along with it has been John's quest and passion. Currently, he teaches workshops, classes, seminars to actors, directors, animators and business professionals around the world and most recently has made his entire curriculum available online for the first time (*emotiontrainingcenter.com*). It is the most comprehensive and deepest dive in online acting classes to date. In addition, he publishes articles in trade papers and blogs and is one of Backstage's expert contributors.

John is available as a speaker, guest lecturer and one-on-one consultant not just for people who want to be better actors, but those in the multiple "face-to-face" sectors of business who need and want to be better and more real and vibrant communicators.

When he has spare time, John be found noodling on his guitar, piano and honing the world's greatest recipe for pesto.

For more info contact: *john@languageoftheface.com*

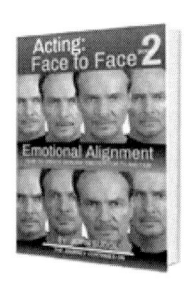

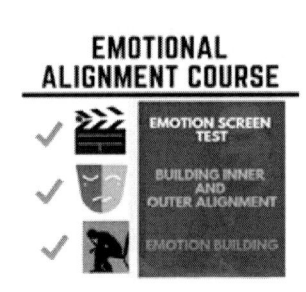

Acknowledgments

This book would not be complete without the acknowledgement of those whose encouragement, contributions and overall hard work made it possible.

First, I want to acknowledge two early pioneers who have contributed enormously to my path. The first, Constantine Stanislavsky, gave me and the world a new way of looking at the actor's process. His relentless commitment put us all on a quest for finding the truth in what we do, say and feel. The other, Dr. Paul Ekman, gave me and the world a greater understanding of emotions, what they are, look like, and feel like. I can only imagine what discoveries Stanislavsky might have made to the craft of on-camera acting had he known of Ekman's work.

There are other scientists that have had a huge impact on my work – far too many to mention here – yet I thank them all. I also want to thank and acknowledge all the great teachers who followed or were influenced by Stanislavsky's work. Their never-ending passion to the understanding of our humanness, our expression, and at times lack of either, has been a driving force not just in this book, but in my life.

I like to thank Lisa Martell for editing the first edition and Leslie Hough and her keen eye for editing the second edition.

I thank Steve Bailin, Anthony Castillo, Caleb Duncan, Emmanuel Fortune, JT Grimm, Sabrina Jones, Hailey Laserna, Katherine Macanufo, Chewie Mon, Jovanna Ortiz, Jordan Preston, and Tamara Rhoads for allowing me to use their photos.

Sincere thanks to all my students, who came into my life and taught me something new each time about how we communicate. I also want to acknowledge all my interns who gave their time and hard work assisting me in so many ways. To of all you, I thank you.

Bibliography

Following is a list of books I have referenced or consulted while creating this work. Since this is a book for actors, I will not list the hundreds of psychological journals or numerous acting and psychology books on my shelves that I've also relied on.

- Ekman, P. & Friesen, W. V. Unmasking the Face: A Guide to Recognizing Emotions from Facial Expressions. Prentice Hall, 2003.
- Ekman, P. Emotions Revealed: Understanding Faces and Feelings. Times Books, 2003.
- Ekman, P. Telling Lies: Clues to Deceit in the Marketplace, Politics, and Marriage. W. W. Norton & Company, 2009.
- Hatfield, E., Cacioppo, J. T., & Rapson, R. L. Emotional Contagion. Cambridge University Press. 1993.
- Matsumoto, D., Frank, M.G. & Hwang, H.S. Nonverbal Communication: Science and Applications. SAGE Publications, 2012.
- Darwin, C. The Expression of Emotion in Man and Animal. D. Appleton and Company, 1873.
- Candace B.P. Molecules of Emotion. Simon & Schuster, 1999.
- Gladwell, M. Blink. Little, Brown and Company, 2005.
- Tucker, P. Secrets of Screen Acting. 2nd ed. Routledge, 2003.

Made in United States
North Haven, CT
08 August 2022